SIGNS &
SEASONS

HARPER NATURE LIBRARY
New Paperback Editions of Outstanding Nature Classics

The Arctic Prairies by Ernest Thompson Seton
  Illustrated by the author

The Arcturus Adventure by William Beebe
  Illustrated

Beyond the Aspen Grove by Ann Zwinger
  Illustrated by the author

The Insect World of J. Henri Fabre edited by Edwin Way Teale

Signs and Seasons by John Burroughs
  Illustrated by Ann Zwinger

The World of Night by Lorus J. and Margery J. Milne
  Illustrated by T. M. Shortt

SIGNS & SEASONS

BY JOHN BURROUGHS

Illustrations by Ann Zwinger

HARPER COLOPHON BOOKS
Harper & Row, Publishers
New York, Cambridge, Hagerstown, Philadelphia, San Francisco
London, Mexico City, São Paulo, Sydney

A hardcover edition of this book was originally published by Houghton Mifflin Company.

SIGNS AND SEASONS. Copyright 1886, 1895, 1914, by John Burroughs. Illustrations copyright © 1981 by Ann Zwinger. All rights reserved. Printed in the United States of America. No part of this book may be used or reproduced in any manner whatsoever without written permission except in the case of brief quotations embodied in critical articles and reviews. For information address Harper & Row, Publishers, Inc., 10 East 53rd Street, New York, N.Y. 10022. Published simultaneously in Canada by Fitzhenry & Whiteside Limited, Toronto.

First HARPER COLOPHON edition published 1981.

ISBN: 0-06-090840-8

81 82 83 84 85 10 9 8 7 6 5 4 3 2 1

CONTENTS

SIGNS &
SEASONS

I

A SHARP LOOKOUT

ONE has only to sit down in the woods or the fields, or by the shore of the river or the lake, and nearly everything of interest will come round to him, — the birds, the animals, the insects; and presently, after his eye has got accustomed to the place, and to the light and shade, he will probably see some plant or flower that he has sought in vain, and that is a pleasant surprise to him. So, on a large scale, the student and lover of nature has this advantage over people who gad up and down the world, seeking some novelty or excitement; he has only to stay at home and see the procession pass. The great globe swings around to him like a revolving showcase; the change of the seasons is like the passage of strange and new countries; the zones of the earth, with all their beauties and marvels, pass one's door, and linger long in the passing. What a voyage is this we make without leaving for a night our own fireside! St. Pierre well says that a sense of the power and mystery of nature shall spring up as fully in one's heart after he has made the circuit of his own field as after returning from a voyage round the world. I sit here amid the junipers of the Hudson, with purpose every year to go to Florida, or to the West Indies, or to the Pacific coast, yet the seasons pass and I am still loitering, with a half-defined suspicion, perhaps, that, if I remain quiet and keep a sharp lookout, these countries will come to me. I may stick it out yet, and not miss much after all. The great trouble is for Mohammed to know when the mountain really comes to him. Sometimes a rabbit or a jay or a little warbler brings the woods to my door. A loon on the river, and the Canada lakes are here; the sea-gulls and the fish hawk bring the sea; the call of the wild gander at night, what does it suggest? and the eagle flapping by, or floating along on a raft of ice, does not he bring the mountain? One spring morning five swans flew above my barn in single file, going north-ward, — an express train bound for Labrador. It was a more exhilarating sight than if I had seen them in their native haunts. They made a breeze in my mind, like a noble passage in a poem. How gently their great wings flapped; how easy to fly when spring gives the impulse! On another occasion I saw a line of fowls, probably swans, going northward, at such a height that they appeared like a faint, waving black line against the sky. They must have been at an altitude of two or three miles.

4

A SHARP LOOKOUT

I was looking intently at the clouds to see which way they moved, when the birds came into my field of vision. I should never have seen them had they not crossed the precise spot upon which my eye was fixed. As it was near sundown, they were probably launched for an all-night pull. They were going with great speed, and as they swayed a little this way and that, they suggested a slender, all but invisible, aerial serpent cleaving the ether. What a highway was pointed out up there! — an easy grade from the Gulf to Hudson's Bay.

Then the typical spring and summer and autumn days, of all shades and complexions, — one cannot afford to miss any of them; and when looked out upon from one's own spot of earth, how much more beautiful and significant they are! Nature comes home to one most when he is at home; the stranger and traveler finds her a stranger and traveler also. One's own landscape comes in time to be a sort of outlying part of himself; he has sowed himself broadcast upon it, and it reflects his own moods and feelings; he is sensitive to the verge of the horizon ; cut those trees, and he bleeds ; mar those hills, and he suffers. How has the farmer planted himself in his fields; builded himself into his stone walls, and evoked the sympathy of the hills by his struggle! This home feeling, this domestication of nature, is important to the observer. This is the bird-lime with which he catches the bird; this is

5

the private door that admits him behind the scenes. This is one source of Gilbert White's charm, and of the charm of Thoreau's " Walden."

The birds that come about one's door in winter, or that build in his trees in summer, what a peculiar interest they have! What crop have I sowed in Florida or in California, that I should go there to reap? I should be only a visitor, or formal caller upon nature, and the family would all wear masks. No; the place to observe nature is where you are; the walk to take to-day is the walk you took yesterday. You will not find just the same things: both the observed and the observer have changed; the ship is on another tack in both cases.

I shall probably never see another just such day as yesterday was, because one can never exactly repeat his observation, — cannot turn the leaf of the book of life backward, — and because each day has characteristics of its own. This was a typical March day, clear, dry, hard, and windy, the river rumpled and crumpled, the sky intense, distant objects strangely near; a day full of strong light, unusual; an extraordinary lightness and clearness all around the horizon, as if there were a diurnal aurora streaming up and burning through the sunlight; smoke from the first spring fires rising up in various directions; a day that winnowed the air, and left no film in the sky. At night, how the big March bellows did work! Venus was like a great lamp in the sky. The stars all seemed brighter than usual, as if the wind blew them up like burning coals. Venus actually seemed to flare in the wind.

Each day foretells the next, if one could read the signs; to-day is the progenitor of to-morrow. When the atmosphere is telescopic, and distant objects stand out unusually clear and sharp, a storm is near. We are on the crest of the wave, and the depression follows quickly. It often happens that clouds are not so indicative of a storm as the total absence of clouds. In this state of the atmosphere the stars are unusually numerous and bright at night, which is also a bad omen.

I find this observation confirmed by Humboldt. " It appears," he says, " that the transparency of the air is prodigiously increased when a certain quantity of water is uniformly diffused through it." Again, he says that the mountaineers of the Alps " predict a change of weather when, the air being calm, the Alps covered with perpetual snow seem on a sudden to be nearer the observer, and their outlines are marked with great distinctness on the azure sky." He further observes that the same condition of the atmosphere renders distant sounds more audible.

There is one redness in the east in the morning that means storm, another that means wind. The former is broad, deep, and angry; the clouds look like a huge bed of burning coals just raked open ;

the latter is softer, more vapory, and more widely extended. Just at the point where the sun is going to rise, and some minutes in advance of his coming, there sometimes rises straight upward a rosy column; it is like a shaft of deeply dyed vapor, blending with and yet partly separated from the clouds, and the base of which presently comes to glow like the sun itself. The day that follows is pretty certain to be very windy. At other times the under sides of the eastern clouds are all turned to pink or rose-colored wool; the transformation extends until nearly the whole sky flushes, even the west glowing slightly; the sign is always to be interpreted as meaning fair weather.

The approach of great storms is seldom heralded by any striking or unusual phenomenon. The real weather gods are free from brag and bluster; but the sham gods fill the sky with portentous signs and omens. I recall one 5th of March as a day that would have filled the ancient observers with dreadful forebodings. At ten o'clock the sun was attended by four extraordinary sun-dogs. A large bright halo encompassed him, on the top of which the segment of a larger circle rested, forming a sort of heavy brilliant crown. At the bottom of the circle, and depending from it, was a mass of soft, glowing, iridescent vapor. On either side, like fragments of the larger circle, were two brilliant arcs. Altogether, it was the most portentous storm-breeding sun I ever beheld. In a dark hemlock wood in a valley, the owls were hooting ominously, and the crows dismally cawing. Before night the storm set in, a little sleet and rain of a few hours' duration, insignificant enough compared with the signs and wonders that preceded it.

To what extent the birds or animals can foretell the weather is uncertain. When the swallows are seen hawking very high, it is a good indication; the insects upon which they feed venture up there only in the most auspicious weather. Yet bees will continue to leave the hive when a storm is imminent. I am told that one of the most reliable weather signs they have down in Texas is afforded by the ants. The ants bring their eggs up out of their underground retreats and expose them to the warmth of the sun to be hatched. When they are seen carrying them in again in great haste, though there be not a cloud in the sky, your walk or your drive must be postponed: a storm is at hand. There is a passage in Virgil that is doubtless intended to embody a similar observation, though none of his translators seem to have hit its meaning accurately: —

"Sæpius et tectis penetralibus extulit ova
        Angustum formica terens iter;"

" Often also has the pismire making a narrow road brought forth her eggs out of the hidden recesses," is the literal translation of old John Martyn.

" Also the ant, incessantly traveling
   The same straight way with the eggs of her hidden
       store,''

is one of the latest metrical translations. Dryden
has it : —

   " The careful ant her secret cell forsakes
     And drags her eggs along the narrow tracks,''

which comes nearer to the fact. When a storm is
coming, Virgil also makes his swallows skim low
about the lake, which agrees with the observation
above.

The critical moments of the day as regards the
weather are at sunrise and sunset. A clear sunset
is always a good sign; an obscured sun, just at the
moment of going down after a bright day, bodes
storm. There is much truth, too, in the saying
that if it rain before seven, it will clear before
eleven. Nine times in ten it will turn out thus.
The best time for it to begin to rain or snow, if it
wants to hold out, is about mid-forenoon. The
great storms usually begin at this time. On all
occasions the weather is very sure to declare itself
before eleven o'clock. If you are going on a pic-
nic, or are going to start on a journey, and the
morning is unsettled, wait till ten and one half
o'clock, and you will know what the remainder
of the day will be. Midday clouds and afternoon
clouds, except in the season of thunderstorms, are

10

usually harmless idlers and vagabonds. But more
to be relied on than any obvious sign is that subtle
perception of the condition of the weather which
a man has who spends much of his time in the
open air. He can hardly tell how he knows it is
going to rain; he hits the fact as an Indian does
the mark with his arrow, without calculating and
by a kind of sure instinct. As you read a man's
purpose in his face, so you learn to read the purpose of the weather in the face of the day.

In observing the weather, however, as in the
diagnosis of disease, the diathesis is all-important.
All signs fail in a drought, because the predispo-
sition, the diathesis, is so strongly toward fair
weather; and the opposite signs fail during a wet
spell, because nature is caught in the other rut.

Observe the lilies of the field. Sir John Lub-
bock says the dandelion lowers itself after flowering,
and lies close to the ground while it is maturing its
seed, and then rises up. It is true that the dandelion lowers itself after flowering, retires from society, as it were, and meditates in seclusion; but
after it lifts itself up again, the stalk begins anew
to grow, it lengthens daily, keeping just above the
grass till the fruit is ripened, and the little globe of
silvery down is carried many inches higher than
was the ring of golden flowers. And the reason is
obvious. The plant depends upon the wind to
scatter its seeds ; every one of these little vessels

spreads a sail to the breeze, and it is necessary that
they be launched above the grass and weeds, amid
which they would be caught and held did the stalk
not continue to grow and outstrip the rival vegetation. It is a curious instance of foresight in a
weed.

I wish I could read as clearly this puzzle of the
button-balls (American plane-tree). Why has Nature taken such particular pains to keep these balls
hanging to the parent tree intact till spring? What
secret of hers has she buttoned in so securely? for
these buttons will not come off. The wind cannot
twist them off, nor warm nor wet hasten or retard
them. The stem, or peduncle, by which the ball
is held in the fall and winter, breaks up into a
dozen or more threads or strands, that are stronger
than those of hemp. When twisted tightly they
make a little cord that I find impossible to break
with my hands. Had they been longer, the Indian
would surely have used them to make his bow-
strings and all the other strings he required. One
could hang himself with a small cord of them. (In
South America, Humboldt saw excellent cordage
made by the Indians from the petioles of the Chi-
quichiqui palm.) Nature has determined that these
buttons should stay on. In order that the seeds of
this tree may germinate, it is probably necessary
that they be kept dry during the winter, and reach
the ground after the season of warmth and moisture

is fully established. In May, just as the leaves and the new balls are emerging, at the touch of a warm, moist south wind, these spherical packages suddenly go to pieces — explode, in fact, like tiny bombshells that were fused to carry to this point — and scatter their seeds to the four winds. They yield at the same time a fine pollen-like dust that one would suspect played some part in fertilizing the new balls, did not botany teach him otherwise. At any rate, it is the only deciduous tree I know of that does not let go the old seed till the new is well on the way. It is plain why the sugar-berry-tree or lotus holds its drupes all winter: it is in order that the birds may come and sow the seed. The berries are like small gravel-stones with a sugar coating, and a bird will not eat them till he is pretty hard pressed, but in late fall and winter the robins, cedar-birds, and bluebirds devour them readily, and of course lend their wings to scatter the seed far and wide. The same is true of juniper-berries, and the fruit of the bitter-sweet.

In certain other cases where the fruit tends to hang on during the winter, as with the bladder-nut and the honey-locust, it is probably because the frost and the perpetual moisture of the ground would rot or kill the germ. To beechnuts, chestnuts, and acorns the moisture of the ground and the covering of leaves seem congenial, though too much warmth and moisture often cause the acorns to germinate prematurely. I have found the ground under the oaks in December covered with nuts, all anchored to the earth by purple sprouts. But the winter which follows such untimely growths generally proves fatal to them.

One must always cross-question nature if he would get at the truth, and he will not get at it then unless he frames his questions with great skill. Most persons are unreliable observers because they put only leading questions, or vague questions.

Perhaps there is nothing in the operations of nature to which we can properly apply the term intelligence, yet there are many things that at first sight look like it. Place a tree or plant in an unusual position and it will prove itself equal to the occasion, and behave in an unusual manner; it will show original resources; it will seem to try intelligently to master the difficulties. Up by Furlow Lake, where I was camping out, a young hemlock had become established upon the end of a large and partly decayed log that reached many feet out into the lake. The young tree was eight or nine feet high; it had sent its roots down into the log and clasped it around on the outside, and had apparently discovered that there was water instead of soil immediately beneath it, and that its sustenance must be sought elsewhere and that quickly. Accordingly it had started one large root, by far the largest of all, for the shore along the top of the log. This root, when I saw the tree, was six or seven feet long, and had bridged more than half the distance that separated the tree from the land.

Was this a kind of intelligence? If the shore had lain in the other direction, no doubt at all but the root would have started for the other side. I know a yellow pine that stands on the side of a steep hill. To make its position more secure, it has thrown out a large root at right angles with its stem directly into the bank above it, which acts as a stay or guy-rope. It was positively the best thing the tree could do. The earth has washed away so that the root where it leaves the tree is two feet above the surface of the soil.

Yet both these cases are easily explained, and without attributing any power of choice, or act of intelligent selection, to the trees. In the case of the little hemlock upon the partly submerged log, roots were probably thrown out equally in all directions; on all sides but one they reached the water and stopped growing; the water checked them; but on the land side, the root on the top of the log, not meeting with any obstacle of the kind, kept on growing, and thus pushing its way toward the shore. It was a case of survival, not of the fittest, but of that which the situation favored, — the fittest with reference to position.

So with the pine-tree on the side of the hill. It probably started its roots in all directions, but only the one on the upper side survived and matured. Those on the lower side finally perished, and others lower down took their places. Thus the whole life upon the globe, as we see it, is the result of this blind groping and putting forth of Nature in every direction, with failure of some of her ventures and the success of others, the circumstances, the environments, supplying the checks and supplying the stimulus, the seed falling upon the barren places just the same as upon the fertile. No discrimination on the part of Nature that we can express in the terms of our own consciousness, but ceaseless experiments in every possible direction. The only thing inexplicable is the inherent impulse to experiment, the original push, the principle of Life.

The good observer of nature holds his eye long and firmly to the point, as one does when looking at a puzzle picture, and will not be baffled. The cat catches the mouse, not merely because she watches for him, but because she is armed to catch him and is quick. So the observer finally gets the fact, not only because he has patience, but because his eye is sharp and his inference swift. Many a shrewd old farmer looks upon the milky way as a kind of weathercock, and will tell you that the way it points at night indicates the direction of the wind the following day. So, also, every new moon is either a dry moon or a wet moon, dry if a powder-horn would hang upon the lower limb, wet if it would not; forgetting the fact that, as a rule, when it is dry in one part of the continent it is wet in some other part, and *vice versa*. When he kills his hogs in the fall, if the pork be very hard and solid, he predicts a severe winter; if soft and loose, the opposite; again overlooking the fact that the kind of food and the temperature of the fall make the pork hard or make it soft. So with a hundred other signs, all the result of hasty and incomplete observations.

One season, the last day of December was very warm. The bees were out of the hive, and there was no frost in the air or in the ground. I was walking in the woods, when as I paused in the shade of a hemlock-tree I heard a sound proceed from beneath the wet leaves on the ground but a few feet from me that suggested a frog. Following it cautiously up, I at last determined upon the exact spot whence the sound issued; lifting up the thick layer of leaves, there sat a frog — the wood frog, one of the first to appear in the marshes in spring, and which I have elsewhere called the " clucking frog " — in a little excavation in the surface of the leaf mould. As it sat there, the top of its back was level with the surface of the ground. This, then, was its hibernaculum; here it was prepared to pass the winter, with only a coverlid of wet matted leaves between it and zero weather. Forthwith I set up as a prophet of warm weather, and among other things predicted a failure of the ice crop on the river; which, indeed, others, who had not heard frogs croak on the 31st of December, had also begun to predict. Surely, I thought, this frog knows what it is about; here is the wisdom of nature; it would have gone deeper into the ground than that if a severe winter was approaching; so I was not anxious about my coal-bin, nor disturbed by longings for Florida. But what a winter followed, the winter of 1885, when the Hudson became coated with ice nearly two feet thick, and when March was as cold as January! I thought of my frog under the hemlock and wondered how it was faring. So one day the latter part of March, when the snow was gone, and there was a feeling of spring in the air, I turned aside in my walk to investigate it. The matted leaves were still frozen hard, but I succeeded in lifting them up and exposing the frog. There it sat as fresh and unscathed as in the fall. The ground beneath and all about it was still frozen like a rock, but apparently it had some means of its own of resisting the frost. It winked and bowed its head when I touched it, but did not seem inclined to leave its retreat. Some days later, after the frost was nearly all out of the ground, I passed that way, and found my frog had come out of its seclusion and was resting amid the dry leaves. There was not much jump in it yet, but its color was growing lighter. A few more warm days, and its fellows, and doubtless itself too, were croaking and gamboling in the marshes.

This incident convinced me of two things; namely, that frogs know no more about the coming weather than we do, and that they do not retreat as deep into the ground to pass the winter as has been supposed. I used to think the muskrats could foretell an early and a severe winter, and have so written. But I am now convinced they cannot; they know as little about it as I do. Sometimes on an early and severe frost they seem to get alarmed and go to building their houses, but usually they seem to build early or late, high or low, just as the whim takes them.

In most of the operations of nature there is at least one unknown quantity; to find the exact value of this unknown factor is not so easy. The wool of the sheep, the fur of the animals, the feathers of the fowls, the husks of the maize, why are they thicker some seasons than others; what is the value of the unknown quantity here? Does it indicate a severe winter approaching? Only observations extending over a series of years could determine the point. How much patient observation it takes to settle many of the facts in the lives of the birds, animals, and insects! Gilbert White was all his life trying to determine whether or not swallows passed the winter in a torpid state in the mud at the bottom of ponds and marshes, and he died ignorant of the truth that they do not. Do honey-bees injure the grape and other fruits by puncturing the skin for the juice? The most patient watching by many skilled eyes all over the country has not yet settled the point. For my own part, I am convinced that they do not. The honey-bee is not the rough-and-ready freebooter that the wasp and the bumblebee are; she has somewhat of feminine timidity, and leaves the first rude assaults to them. I knew the honey-bee was very fond of the locust blossoms, and that the trees hummed like a hive in the height of their flowering, but I did not know that the bumblebee was ever the sapper and miner that went ahead in this enterprise, till one day I placed myself amid the foliage of a locust and saw him savagely bite through the shank of the flower and extract the nectar, followed by a honey-bee that in every instance searched for this opening, and probed long and carefully for the leavings of her burly purveyor. The bumblebee rifles the dicentra and the columbine of their treasures in the same manner, namely, by slitting their pockets from the outside, and the honey-bee gleans after him, taking the small change he leaves. In the case of the locust, however, she usually obtains the honey without the aid of the larger bee.

Speaking of the honey-bee reminds me that the subtle and sleight-of-hand manner in which she fills her baskets with pollen and propolis is character-

istic of much of Nature's doings. See the bee
going from flower to flower with the golden pellets
on her thighs, slowly and mysteriously increasing
in size. If the miller were to take the toll of the
grist he grinds by gathering the particles of flour
from his coat and hat, as he moved rapidly about,
or catching them in his pockets, he would be doing
pretty nearly what the bee does. The little miller
dusts herself with the pollen of the flower, and
then, while on the wing, brushes it off with the
fine brush on certain of her feet, and by some jug-
glery or other catches it in her pollen basket. One
needs to look long and intently to see through the
trick. Pliny says they fill their baskets with their
fore feet, and that they fill their fore feet with
their trunks, but it is a much more subtle operation
than this. I have seen the bees come to a meal
barrel in early spring, and to a pile of hardwood
sawdust before there was yet anything in nature for
them to work upon, and, having dusted their coats
with the finer particles of the meal or the sawdust,
hover on the wing above the mass till the little
legerdemain feat was performed. Nature fills her
baskets by the same sleight-of-hand, and the observer must be on the alert who would possess her
secret. If the ancients had looked a little closer
and sharper, would they ever have believed in
spontaneous generation in the superficial way in
which they did ; that maggots, for instance, were gen-

erated spontaneously in putrid flesh? Could they
not see the spawn of the blow-flies? Or, if Virgil
had been a real observer of the bees, would he ever
have credited, as he certainly appears to do, the
fable of bees originating from the carcass of a steer?
or that on windy days they carried little stones for
ballast? or that two hostile swarms fought each
other in the air? Indeed, the ignorance, or the
false science, of the ancient observers, with regard
to the whole subject of bees, is most remarkable;
not false science merely with regard to their more
hidden operations, but with regard to that which
is open and patent to all who have eyes in their
heads, and have ever had to do with them. And
Pliny names authors who had devoted their whole
lives to the study of the subject.

But the ancients, like women and children, were
not accurate observers. Just at the critical moment
their eyes were unsteady, or their fancy, or their
credulity, or their impatience, got the better of
them, so that their science was half fact and half
fable. Thus, for instance, because the young cuckoo
at times appeared to take the head of its small
foster mother quite into its mouth while receiving
its food, they believed that it finally devoured her.
Pliny, who embodied the science of his times in
his natural history, says of the wasp that it carries
spiders to its nest, and then sits upon them until
it hatches its young from them. A little careful

observation would have shown him that this was only a half truth; that the whole truth was, that the spiders were entombed with the egg of the wasp to serve as food for the young when the egg had hatched.

What curious questions Plutarch discusses, as, for instance, "What is the reason that a bucket of water drawn out of a well, if it stands all night in the air that is in the well, is more cold in the morning than the rest of the water?" He could probably have given many reasons why "a watched pot never boils." The ancients, the same author says, held that the bodies of those killed by lightning never putrefy; that the sight of a ram quiets an enraged elephant; that a viper will lie stock-still if touched by a beechen leaf; that a wild bull grows tame if bound with the twigs of a fig-tree; that a hen purifies herself with straw after she has laid an egg; that the deer buries his cast-off horns; and that a goat stops the whole herd by holding a branch of the sea-holly in his mouth. They sought to account for such things without stopping to ask, Are they true? Nature was too novel, or else too fearful, to them to be deliberately pursued and hunted down. Their youthful joy in her, or their dread and awe in her presence, may be better than our scientific satisfaction, or cool wonder, or our vague, mysterious sense of "something far more deeply interfused;" yet we cannot change

with them if we would, and I, for one, would not if
I could. Science does not mar nature. The railroad,
Thoreau found, after all, to be about the wildest
road he knew of, and the telegraph wires the best
æolian harp out of doors. Study of nature deepens
the mystery and the charm because it removes the
horizon farther off. We cease to fear, perhaps, but
how can one cease to marvel and to love?

The fields and woods and waters about one are
a book from which he may draw exhaustless enter-
tainment, if he will. One must not only learn
the writing, he must translate the language, the
signs, and the hieroglyphics. It is a very quaint
and elliptical writing, and much must be supplied
by the wit of the translator. At any rate, the les-
son is to be well conned. Gilbert White said that
that locality would be found the richest in zoölo-
gical or botanical specimens which was most
thoroughly examined. For more than forty years
he studied the ornithology of his district without
exhausting the subject. I thought I knew my own
tramping-ground pretty well, but one April day,
when I looked a little closer than usual into a small
semi-stagnant lakelet where I had peered a hundred
times before, I suddenly discovered scores of little
creatures that were as new to me as so many
nymphs would have been. They were partly fish-
shaped, from an inch to an inch and a half long,
semi-transparent, with a dark brownish line visible

the entire length of them (apparently the thread upon which the life of the animal hung, and by which its all but impalpable frame was held together), and suspending themselves in the water, or impelling themselves swiftly forward by means of a double row of fine, waving, hair-like appendages, that arose from what appeared to be the back, — a kind of undulating, pappus-like wings. What was it? I did not know. None of my friends or scientific acquaintances knew. I wrote to a learned man, an authority upon fish, describing the creature as well as I could. He replied that it was only a familiar species of phyllopodous crustacean, known as *Eubranchipus vernalis.*

I remember that our guide in the Maine woods, seeing I had names of my own for some of the plants, would often ask me the name of this and that flower for which he had no word ; and that when I could recall the full Latin term, it seemed overwhelmingly convincing and satisfying to him. It was evidently a relief to know that these obscure plants of his native heath had been found worthy of a learned name, and that the Maine woods were not so uncivil and outlandish as they might at first seem: it was a comfort to him to know that he did not live beyond the reach of botany. In like manner I found satisfaction in knowing that my novel fish had been recognized and worthily named; the title conferred a new dignity at once; but when the

learned man added that it was familiarly called the
" fairy shrimp," I felt a deeper pleasure. Fairy-
like it certainly was, in its aerial, unsubstantial
look, and in its delicate, down-like means of loco-
motion; but the large head, with its curious folds,
and its eyes standing out in relief, as if on the
heads of two pins, was gnome-like. Probably the
fairy wore a mask, and wanted to appear terrible
to human eyes. Then the creatures had sprung out
of the earth as by magic. I found some in a fur-
row in a plowed field that had encroached upon a
swamp. In the fall the plow had been there, and
had turned up only the moist earth ; now a little
water was standing there, from which the April
sunbeams had invoked these airy, fairy creatures.
They belong to the crustaceans, but apparently no
creature has so thin or impalpable a crust; you can
almost see through them ; certainly you can see
what they have had for dinner, if they have eaten
substantial food.

All we know about the private and essential
natural history of the bees, the birds, the fishes,
the animals, the plants, is the result of close, patient, quick-witted observation. Yet Nature will
often elude one for all his pains and alertness.
Thoreau, as revealed in his journal, was for years
trying to settle in his own mind what was the first
thing that stirred in spring, after the severe New
England winter, — in what was the first sign or

pulse of returning life manifest; and he never seems to have been quite sure. He could not get his salt on the tail of this bird. He dug into the swamps, he peered into the water, he felt with benumbed hands for the radical leaves of the plants under the snow; he inspected the buds on the willows, the catkins on the alders; he went out before daylight of a March morning and remained out after dark; he watched the lichens and mosses on the rocks; he listened for the birds; he was on the alert for the first frog (" Can you be absolutely sure," he says, " that you have heard the first frog that croaked in the township? "); he stuck a pin here and he stuck a pin there, and there, and still he could not satisfy himself. Nor can any one. Life appears to start in several things simultaneously. Of a warm thawy day in February the snow is suddenly covered with myriads of snow fleas looking like black, new powder just spilled there. Or you may see a winged insect in the air. On the selfsame day the grass in the spring run and the catkins on the alders will have started a little; and if you look sharply, while passing along some sheltered nook or grassy slope where the sunshine lies warm on the bare ground, you will probably see a grasshopper or two. The grass hatches out under the snow, and why should not the grasshopper? At any rate, a few such hardy specimens may be found in the latter part of our milder winters wherever the sun has uncovered a sheltered bit of grass for a few days, even after a night of ten or twelve degrees of frost. Take them in the shade, and let them freeze stiff as pokers, and when thawed out again they will hop briskly. And yet, if a poet were to put grasshoppers in his winter poem, we should require pretty full specifications of him, or else fur to clothe them with. Nature will not be cornered, yet she does many things in a corner and surreptitiously. She is all things to all men; she has whole truths, half truths, and quarter truths, if not still smaller fractions. The careful observer finds this out sooner or later. Old fox-hunters will tell you, on the evidence of their own eyes, that there is a black fox and a silver-gray fox, two species, but there are not ; the black fox is black when coming toward you or running from you, and silver gray at point-blank view, when the eye penetrates the fur; each separate hair is gray the first half and black the last. This is a sample of Nature's half truths.

Which are our sweet-scented wild flowers ? Put your nose to every flower you pluck, and you will be surprised how your list will swell the more you smell. I plucked some wild blue violets one day, the *ovata* variety of the *sagittata*, that had a faint perfume of sweet clover, but I never could find another that had any odor. A pupil disputed with his teacher about the hepatica, claiming in opposition that it was sweet-scented. Some hepaticas are sweet-scented and some are not, and the perfume is stronger some seasons than others. After the unusually severe winter of 1880–81, the variety of hepatica called the sharp-lobed was markedly sweet in nearly every one of the hundreds of specimens I examined. A handful of them exhaled a most delicious perfume. The white ones that season were largely in the ascendant ; and probably the white specimens of both varieties, one season with another, will oftenest prove sweet-scented. Darwin says a considerably larger proportion of white flowers are sweet-scented than of any other color. The only sweet violets I can depend upon are white, *Viola blanda* and *Viola Canadensis*, and white largely predominates among our other odorous wild flowers. All the fruit trees have white or pinkish blossoms. I recall no native blue flower of New York or New England that is fragrant except in the rare case of the arrow-leaved violet, above referred to. The earliest yellow flowers, like the dandelion and yellow violets, are not fragrant. Later in the season yellow is frequently accompanied with fragrance, as in the evening primrose, the yellow lady's-slipper, horned bladderwort, and others.

My readers probably remember that on a former occasion I have mildly taken the poet Bryant to task for leading his readers to infer that the early yellow violet is sweet-scented. In view of the capriciousness of the perfume of certain of our wild flowers, I have during the past few years tried industriously to convict myself of error in respect to this flower. The round-leaved yellow violet was one of the earliest and most abundant wild flowers in the woods where my youth was passed, and whither I still make annual pilgrimages. I have pursued it on mountains and in lowlands, in "beechen woods" and amid the hemlocks; and while, with respect to its earliness, it overtakes the hepatica in the latter part of April, as do also the dog's-tooth violet and the claytonia, yet the first hepaticas, where the two plants grow side by side, bloom about a week before the first violet. And I have yet to find one that has an odor that could be called a perfume. A handful of them, indeed, has a faint, bitterish smell, not unlike that of the dandelion in quality; but if every flower that has a smell is sweet-scented, then every bird that makes a noise is a songster.

On the occasion above referred to, I also dissented from Lowell's statement, in "Al Fresco," that in early summer the dandelion blooms, in general, with the buttercup and the clover. I am aware that such criticism of the poets is small game, and not worth the powder. General truth, and not specific fact, is what we are to expect of the poets. Bryant's "Yellow Violet" poem is tender and appropriate, and such as only a real lover and ob-

server of nature could feel or express; and Lowell's
"Al Fresco" is full of the luxurious feeling of early
summer, and this is, of course, the main thing; a
good reader cares for little else; I care for little else
myself. But when you take your coin to the assay
office, it must be weighed and tested, and in the
comments referred to I (unwisely, perhaps) sought
to smelt this gold of the poets in the naturalist's
pot, to see what alloy of error I could detect in it.
Were the poems true to their last word? They were
not, and much subsequent investigation has only
confirmed my first analysis. The general truth is on
my side, and the specific fact, if such exists in this
case, on the side of the poets. It is possible that
there may be a fragrant yellow violet, as an exceptional occurrence, like that of the sweet-scented,
arrow-leaved species above referred to, and that in
some locality it may have bloomed before the hepatica; also that Lowell may have seen a belated
dandelion or two in June, amid the clover and the
buttercups; but, if so, they were the exception, and
not the rule, — the specific or accidental fact, and
not the general truth.

Dogmatism about nature, or about anything else,
very often turns out to be an ungrateful cur that
bites the hand that reared it. I speak from experience. I was once quite certain that the honey-
bee did not work upon the blossoms of the trailing
arbutus, but while walking in the woods one April

day I came upon a spot of arbutus swarming with honey-bees. They were so eager for it that they crawled under the leaves and the moss to get at the blossoms, and refused on the instant the hive-honey which I happened to have with me, and which I offered them. I had had this flower under observation more than twenty years, and had never before seen it visited by honey-bees. The same season I saw them for the first time working upon the flower of bloodroot and of adder's-tongue. Hence I would not undertake to say again what flowers bees do not work upon. Virgil implies that they work upon the violet, and for aught I know they may. I have seen them very busy on the blossoms of the white oak, though this is not considered a honey or pollen yielding tree. From the smooth sumac they reap a harvest in midsummer, and in March they get a good grist of pollen from the skunk-cabbage.

I presume, however, it would be safe to say that there is a species of smilax with an unsavory name that the bee does not visit, *Smilax herbacea.* The production of this plant is a curious freak of nature. I find it growing along the fences where one would look for wild roses or the sweetbrier ; its recurving or climbing stem, its glossy, deep-green, heart-shaped leaves, its clustering umbels of small greenish yellow flowers, making it very pleasing to the eye; but to examine it closely one must positively hold his nose. It would be too cruel a joke to offer it to any person not acquainted with it to smell. It is like the vent of a charnel-house. It is first cousin to the trilliums, among the prettiest of our native wild flowers, and the same bad blood crops out in the purple trillium or birthroot.

Nature will include the disagreeable and repulsive also. I have seen the phallic fungus growing in June under a rosebush. There was the rose, and beneath it, springing from the same mould, was this diabolical offering to Priapus. With the perfume of the roses into the open window came the stench of this hideous parody, as if in mockery. I removed it, and another appeared in the same place shortly afterward. The earthman was rampant and insulting. Pan is not dead yet. At least he still makes a ghastly sign here and there in nature.

The good observer of nature exists in fragments, a trait here and a trait there. Each person sees what it concerns him to see. The fox-hunter knows pretty well the ways and habits of the fox, but on any other subject he is apt to mislead you. He comes to see only fox traits in whatever he looks upon. The bee-hunter will follow the bee, but lose the bird. The farmer notes what affects his crops and his earnings, and little else. Common people, St. Pierre says, observe without reasoning, and the learned reason without observing. If one could apply to the observation of nature the sense and skill of the South American *rastreador*, or trailer, how much he would track home! This man's eye, according to the accounts of travelers, is keener than a hound's scent. A fugitive can no more elude him than he can elude fate. His perceptions are said to be so keen that the displacement of a leaf or pebble, or the bending down of a spear of grass, or the removal of a little dust from the fence, is enough to give him the clew. He sees the half-obliterated footprints of a thief in the sand, and carries the impression in his eye till a year afterward, when he again detects the same footprint in the suburbs of a city, and the culprit is tracked home and caught. I knew a man blind from his youth who not only went about his own neighborhood without a guide, turning up to his neighbor's gate or door as unerringly as if he had the best of eyes, but who would go many miles on an errand to a new part of the country. He seemed to carry a map of the township in the bottom of his feet, a most minute and accurate survey. He never took the wrong road, and he knew the right house when he had reached it. He was a miller and fuller, and ran his mill at night while his sons ran it by day. He never made a mistake with his customers' bags or wool, knowing each man's by the sense of touch. He frightened a colored man whom he detected stealing, as if he had seen out of the back of his head. Such facts show one how delicate and sensitive a man's relation to outward nature through his bodily senses may become. Heighten it a little more, and he could forecast the weather and the seasons, and detect hidden springs and minerals. A good observer has something of this delicacy and quickness of perception. All the great poets and naturalists have it. Agassiz traces the glaciers like a *rastreador ;* and Darwin misses no step that the slow but tireless gods of physical change have taken, no matter how they cross or retrace their course. In the obscure fish-worm he sees an agent that has kneaded and leavened the soil like giant hands.

One secret of success in observing nature is capacity to take a hint ; a hair may show where a lion is hid. One must put this and that together, and value bits and shreds. Much alloy exists with the truth. The gold of nature does not look like gold at the first glance. It must be smelted and refined in the mind of the observer. And one must crush mountains of quartz and wash hills of sand to get it. To know the indications is the main matter. People who do not know the secret are eager to take a walk with the observer to find where the mine is that contains such nuggets, little knowing that his ore-bed is but a gravel-heap to them. How insignificant appear most of the facts which one sees in his walks, in the life of the birds, the flowers, the animals, or in the phases of the landscape, or the look of the sky!—insignificant until they are put through some mental or emotional process and their true value appears. The diamond looks like a pebble until it is cut. One goes to Nature only for hints and half truths. Her facts are crude until you have absorbed them or translated them. Then the ideal steals in and lends a charm in spite of one. It is not so much what we see as what the thing seen suggests. We all see about the same ; to one it means much, to another little. A fact that has passed through the mind of man, like lime or iron that has passed through his blood, has some quality or property superadded or brought out that it did not possess before. You may go to the fields and the woods, and gather fruit that is ripe for the palate without any aid of yours, but you cannot do this in science or in art. Here truth must be disentangled and interpreted, — must be made in the image of man. Hence all good observation is more or less a refining and transmuting process, and the secret is to know the crude material when you see it. I think of Wordsworth's lines:—

> "The mighty world
> Of eye and ear, both what they half create, and what
> perceive;"

which is as true in the case of the naturalist as of the poet; both "half create" the world they describe.

A SHARP LOOKOUT

Darwin does something to his facts as well as Tennyson to his. Before a fact can become poetry, it must pass through the heart or the imagination of the poet; before it can become science, it must pass through the understanding of the scientist. Or one may say, it is with the thoughts and half thoughts that the walker gathers in the woods and fields, as with the common weeds and coarser wild flowers which he plucks for a bouquet, — wild carrot, purple aster, moth mullein, sedge, grass, etc. : they look common and uninteresting enough there in the fields, but the moment he separates them from the tangled mass, and brings them indoors, and places them in a vase, say of some choice glass, amid artificial things, — behold, how beautiful! They have an added charm and significance at once; they are defined and identified, and what was common and familiar becomes unexpectedly attractive. The writer's style, the quality of mind he brings, is the vase in which his commonplace impressions and incidents are made to appear so beautiful and significant.

Man can have but one interest in nature, namely, to see himself reflected or interpreted there, and we quickly neglect both poet and philosopher who fail to satisfy, in some measure, this feeling.

II

A SPRAY OF PINE

HOW different the expression of the pine, in fact of all the coniferæ, from that of the deciduous trees! Not different merely by reason of color and foliage, but by reason of form. The deciduous trees have greater diversity of shapes; they tend to branch endlessly; they divide and subdivide until the original trunk is lost in a maze of limbs. Not so the pine and its congeners. Here the main thing is the central shaft; there is one dominant shoot which leads all the rest, and which points the tree upward; the original type is never departed from: the branches shoot out at nearly right angles to the trunk, and occur in regular whorls; the main stem is never divided unless some accident nips the leading shoot, when two secondary branches will often rise up and lead the tree forward. The pine has no power to develop new buds, new shoots, like the deciduous trees; no power of spontaneous variation to meet new exigencies, new requirements. It is, as it were, cast in a mould. Its buds, its branches, occur in regular series and after a regular pattern. Interrupt this series, try to vary this pattern, and the tree is powerless to adapt itself to any other. Victor Hugo, in his old age, compared himself to a tree that had been many times cut down, but which always sprouted again. But the pines do not sprout again. The spontaneous development of a new bud or a new shoot rarely or never occurs. The hemlock seems to be under the same law. I have cut away all the branches, and rubbed away all the buds, of a young sapling of this species, and found the tree, a year and a half later, full of life, but with no leaf or bud upon it. It could not break the spell. One bud would have released it and set its currents going again, but it was powerless to develop it. Remove the bud, or the new growth from the end of the central shaft of the branch of a pine, and in a year or two the branch will die back to the next joint; remove the whorl of branches here, and it will die back to the next whorl, and so on.

When you cut the top of a pine or a spruce, removing the central and leading shaft, the tree does not develop and send forth a new one to take the place of the old, but a branch from the next in rank, that is, from the next whorl of limbs, is promoted to take the lead. It is curious to witness this limb rise up and get into position. One season I cut off the tops of some young hemlocks that were about ten feet high, that I had balled in the winter and had moved into position for a hedge.

The next series of branches consisted of three that shot out nearly horizontally. As time passed, one of these branches, apparently the most vigorous, began to lift itself up very slowly toward the place occupied by the lost leader. The third year it stood at an angle of about forty-five degrees ; the fourth year it had gained about half the remaining distance, when the clipping shears again cut it down. In five years it would probably have assumed an upright position. A white pine of about the same height lost its central shaft by a grub that developed from the egg of an insect, and I cut it away. It rose from a whorl of four branches, and it now devolved upon one of these to take the lead. Two of them, on opposite sides, were more vigorous than the other two, and the struggle now is as to which of these two shall gain the mastery. Both are rising up and turning toward the vacant chieftainship, and, unless something interferes, the tree will probably become forked and led upward by two equal branches. I shall probably humble the pride of one of the rivals by nipping its central shoot. One of my neighbors has cut off a yellow pine about six inches in diameter, so as to leave only one circle of limbs seven or eight feet from the ground. It is now the third year of the tree's decapitation, and one of this circle of horizontal limbs has risen up several feet, like a sleeper rising from his couch, and seems to be looking around inquiringly, as much as to say:

"Come, brothers, wake up! Some one must take the lead here; shall it be I?"

In one of my Norway spruces I have witnessed the humbling or reducing to the ranks of a would-be leading central shoot. For a couple of years the vigorous young tree was led upward by two rival branches; they appeared almost evenly matched; but on the third year one of them clearly took the lead, and at the end of the season was a foot or more in advance of the other. The next year the distance between them became still greater, and the defeated leader appeared to give up the contest, so that a season or two afterward it began to lose its upright attitude and to fall more and more toward a horizontal position; it was willing to go back into the ranks of the lateral branches. Its humiliation was so great that it even for a time dropped below them; but toward midsummer it lifted up its head a little, and was soon fairly in the position of a side branch, simulating defeat and willing subordination as completely as if it had been a conscious, sentient being.

The evergreens can keep a secret the year round, some one has said. How well they keep the secret of the shedding of their leaves! so well that in the case of the spruces we hardly know when it does occur. In fact, the spruces do not properly shed their leaves at all, but simply outgrow them, after carrying them an indefinite time. Some of the species carry their leaves five or six years. The hemlock drops its leaves very irregularly : the winds and the storms whip them off; in winter the snow beneath them is often covered with them.

But the pine sheds its leaves periodically, though always as it were stealthily and under cover of the newer foliage. The white pine usually sheds its leaves in midsummer, though I have known all the pines to delay till October. It is on with the new love before it is off with the old. From May till near autumn it carries two crops of leaves, last year's and the present year's. Emerson's inquiry,

> " How the sacred pine-tree adds
>   To her old leaves new myriads,''

is framed in strict accordance with the facts. It is to her *old* leaves that she adds the new. Only the new growth, the outermost leaves, is carried over till the next season, thus keeping the tree always clothed and green. As its moulting season approaches, these old leaves, all the rear ranks on the limbs, begin to turn yellow, and a careless observer might think the tree was struck with death, but it is not. The decay stops just where the growth of the previous spring began, and presently the tree stands green and vigorous, with a newly laid carpet of fallen leaves beneath it.

I wonder why it is that the pine has an ancient look, a suggestion in some way of antiquity? Is

it because we know it to be the oldest tree? or
is it not rather that its repose, its silence, its un-
changeableness, suggest the past, and cause it to
stand out in sharp contrast upon the background
of the flitting, fugitive present? It has such a look
of permanence! When growing from the rocks, it
seems expressive of the same geologic antiquity
as they. It has the simplicity of primitive things;
the deciduous trees seem more complex, more heterogeneous; they have greater versatility, more
resources. The pine has but one idea, and that is
to mount heavenward by regular steps, — tree of
fate, tree of dark shadows and of mystery.

The pine is the tree of silence. Who was the
Goddess of Silence? Look for her altars amid the
pines, — silence above, silence below. Pass from
deciduous woods into pine woods of a windy day,
and you think the day has suddenly become calm.
Then how silent to the foot! One walks over a
carpet of pine needles almost as noiselessly as over
the carpets of our dwellings. Do these halls lead
to the chambers of the great, that all noise should
be banished from them? Let the designers come
here and get the true pattern for a carpet, — a soft
yellowish brown with only a red leaf, or a bit of
gray moss, or a dusky lichen scattered here and
there; a background that does not weary or bewil-
der the eye, or insult the ground-loving foot.

How friendly the pine-tree is to man, — so

docile and available as timber, and so warm and protective as shelter! Its balsam is salve to his wounds, its fragrance is long life to his nostrils; an abiding, perennial tree, tempering the climate, cool as murmuring waters in summer and like a wrapping of fur in winter.

The deciduous trees are inconstant friends that fail us when adverse winds do blow; but the pine and all its tribe look winter cheerily in the face, tossing the snow, masquerading in his arctic livery, in fact holding high carnival from fall to spring. The Norseman of the woods, lofty and aspiring, tree without bluster or noise, that sifts the howling storm into a fine spray of sound; symmetrical tree, tapering, columnar, shaped as in a lathe, the preordained mast of ships, the mother of colossal timbers; centralized, towering, patriarchal, coming down from the foreworld, counting centuries in thy rings and outlasting empires in thy decay.

A little tall talk seems not amiss on such a subject. The American or white pine has been known to grow to a height of two hundred and sixty feet, slender and tapering as a rush, and equally available for friction matches or for the mast of a ship of the line. It is potent upon the sea and upon the land, and lends itself to become a standard for giants or a toy for babes, with equal readiness. No other tree so widely useful in the mechanic arts, or so beneficent in the economy of nature. House of refuge for the winter birds, and inn and hostelry for the spring and fall emigrants. All the northern creatures are more or less dependent upon the pine. Nature has made a singular exception in the conformation of the beaks of certain birds, that they may the better feed upon the seeds of its cones, as in the crossbills. Then the pine grosbeak and pine linnet are both nurslings of this tree. Certain of the warblers, also, the naturalist seldom finds except amid its branches.

The dominant races come from the region of the pine.

> " Who liveth by the ragged pine
> Foundeth a heroic line;"

says Emerson.

> " Who liveth in the palace hall
> Waneth fast and spendeth all. "

The pines of Norway and Sweden sent out the vikings, and out of the pine woods of northern Europe came the virile barbarian overrunning the effete southern countries.

> " And grant to dwellers with the pine
> Dominion o'er the palm and vine."

There is something sweet and piny about the northern literatures as contrasted with those of the voluble and passionate south, — something in them that heals the mind's hurts like a finer balsam. In reading Björnson, or Andersen, or Russian Turgé-neff, though one may not be in contact with the master spirits of the world, he is yet inhaling an atmosphere that is resinous and curative; he is under an influence that is arboreal, temperate, balsamic.

"The white pine," says Wilson Flagg in his "Woods and By-Ways of New England," "has no legendary history. Being an American tree, it is celebrated neither in poetry nor romance." Not perhaps in Old World poetry and romance, but certainly in that of the New World. The New England poets have not overlooked the pine, however much they may have gone abroad for their themes and tropes. Whittier's "My Playmate" is written to the low monotone of the pine.

> "The pines were dark on Ramoth hill,
> Their song was soft and low;
> The blossoms in the sweet May wind
> Were falling like the snow."

Lowell's "To a Pine-Tree" is well known, —

> "Far up on Katahdin thou towerest
> Purple-blue with the distance and vast;
> Like a cloud o'er the lowlands thou lowerest,
> That hangs poised on a lull in the blast
> To its fall leaning awful."

In his "A Mood," his attention is absorbed by

this tree, and in the poet's quest of the muse he says, —

> " I haunt the pine-dark solitudes,
> With soft brown silence carpeted."

But the real white pine among our poets is Emerson. Against that rustling deciduous background of the New England poets he shows dark and aspiring. Emerson seems to have a closer fellowship with the pine than with any other tree, and it recurs again and again in his poems. In his " Garden " the pine is the principal vegetable, — "the snow-loving pines," as he so aptly says, and "the hemlocks tall, untamable." It is perhaps from the pine that he gets the idea that " Nature loves the number five;" its leaves are in fives and its whorl of branches is composed of five. His warbler is the " pine warbler," and he sees " the pigeons in the pines," where they are seldom to be seen. He even puts a " pine state-house " in his " Boston Hymn."

But, more than that, his " Woodnotes," one of his longest poems, is mainly the notes of the pine. Theodore Parker said that a tree that talked like Emerson's pine ought to be cut down; but if the pine were to find a tongue, I should sooner expect to hear the Emersonian dialect from it than almost any other. It would be pretty high up, certainly, and go over the heads of most of the other trees. It were sure to be pointed, though the point few could see. And it would not be garrulous and loud-mouthed, though it might talk on and on. Whether it would preach or not is a question, but I have no doubt it would be a fragrant healing gospel if it did. I think its sentences would be short ones with long pauses between them, and that they would sprout out of the subject independently and not connect or interlock very much. There would be breaks and chasms or maybe some darkness between the lines, but I should expect from it a lofty, cheerful, and all-the-year-round philosophy. The temptation to be oracular would no doubt be great, and could be more readily overlooked in this tree than in any other. Then, the pine being the oldest tree, great wisdom and penetration might be expected of it.

Though Emerson's pine boasts

> " My garden is the cloven rock,
>   And my manure the snow;
>   And drifting sand-heaps feed my stock,
>   In summer's scorching glow," —

yet the great white pine loves a strong deep soil. How it throve along our river bottom and pointed out the best land to the early settlers! Remnants of its stumps are still occasionally seen in land that has been given to the plow these seventy or eighty years. In Pennsylvania the stumps are wrenched from the ground by machinery and used largely for fencing. Laid upon their side, with their wide branching roots in the air, they form a barrier before which even the hound-pursued deer may well pause.

This aboriginal tree is fast disappearing from the country. Its second growth seems to be a degenerate race, what the carpenters contemptuously call pumpkin pine, on account of its softness. All the large tracts and provinces of the original tree have been invaded and ravished by the lumbermen, so that only isolated bands, and straggling specimens, like the remnants of a defeated and disorganized army, are now found scattered up and down the country. The spring floods on our northern rivers have for decades of years been moving seething walls of pine logs, sweeping down out of the wilderness. I remember pausing beside a mammoth pine in the Adirondack woods, standing a little to one side of the destroyer's track, that must have carried its green crown near one hundred and fifty feet above the earth. How such a tree impresses one! How it swells at the base and grows rigid as if with muscular effort in its determined gripe of the earth! How it lays hold of the rocks, or rends them asunder to secure its hold! Nearly all trunk, it seems to have shed its limbs like youthful follies as it went skyward, or as the builders pull down their scaffoldings and carry them higher as the temple mounts; nothing superfluous, no waste of time or energy, the one purpose to cleave the empyrean steadily held to.

At the Centennial fair I saw a section of a pine from Canada that was eight feet in diameter, and that had been growing, I have forgotten how many centuries. But this was only a sapling beside the redwoods of California, one of which would carry several such trees in his belt.

In the absence of the pine, the hemlock is a graceful and noble tree. In primitive woods it shoots up in the same manner, drawing the ladder up after it, and attains an altitude of nearly or quite a hundred feet. It is the poor man's pine, and destined to humbler uses than its lordlier brother. It follows the pine like a servitor, keeping on higher and more rocky ground, and going up the minor branch valleys when the pine follows only the main or mother stream. As an ornamental tree it is very pleasing, and deserves to be cultivated more than it is. It is a great favorite with the sylvan folk, too. The ruffed grouse prefer it to the pine; it is better shelter in winter, and its buds are edible. The red squirrel has found out the seeds in its cones, and they are an important part of his winter stores. Some of the rarer warblers, too, like the Blackburnian and the blue yellow-back, I never find except among the hemlocks. The older ornithologists, Audubon and Wilson, named a " hemlock warbler " also, but this bird turns out to be none other than

51

the young of the Blackburnian described as a new species and named for its favorite tree.

All trees in primitive woods are less social, less disposed to intermingle, than trees in groves or fields: they are more heady; they meet only on high grounds; they shake hands over the heads of their neighbors; the struggle for life is sharper and more merciless, — in these and other respects suggesting men in cities. One tree falls against a more stanch one, and bruises only itself; a weaker one it carries to the ground with it.

Both the pine and the hemlock make friends with the birch, the maple, and the oak, and one of the most pleasing and striking features of our autumnal scenery is a mountain-side sown broadcast with these intermingled trees, forming a combination of colors like the richest tapestry, the dark green giving body and permanence, the orange and yellow giving light and brilliancy.

III

HARD FARE

SUCH a winter as was that of 1880–81 — deep snows and zero weather for nearly three months — proves especially trying to the wild creatures that attempt to face it. The supply of fat (or fuel) with which their bodies become stored in the fall is rapidly exhausted by the severe and uninterrupted cold, and the sources from which fresh supplies are usually obtained are all but wiped out. Even the fox was very hard pressed and reduced to the unusual straits of eating frozen apples; the pressure of hunger must be great, indeed, to compel Reynard to take up with such a diet. A dog will eat corn, but he cannot digest it, and I doubt if the fox extracted anything more than the cider from the frozen and thawed apples. They perhaps served to amuse and occupy his stomach for the time. Humboldt says wolves eat earth, especially clay, during winter, and Pliny makes a similar observation. In Greenland the dog eats seaweed when other food fails. In tropical countries, during the tropical winter, many savage tribes eat clay. It distends their stomachs, and in a measure satisfies the crav-

53

ings of hunger. During the season referred to, the crows appeared to have little else than frozen apples for many weeks; they hung about the orchards as a last resort, and, after scouring the desolate landscape over, would return to their cider with resignation, but not with cheerful alacrity. They grew very bold at times, and ventured quite under my porch, and filched the bones that Lark, the dog, had left. I put out some corn on the wall near by, and discovered that crows will not eat corn in the winter, except as they can break up the kernels. It is too hard for their gizzards to grind. Then the crow, not being properly a granivorous bird, but a carnivorous, has not the digestive, or rather the pulverizing power of the domestic fowls. The difficulty also during such a season of coming at the soil and obtaining gravel-stones, which, in such cases, are really the millstones, may also have something to do with it. Corn that has been planted and has sprouted, crows will swallow readily enough, because it is then soft, and is easily ground. My impression has always been that in spring and summer they will also pick up any chance kernels the planters may have dropped. But, as I observed them the past winter, they always held the kernel under one foot upon the wall, and picked it to pieces before devouring it. This is the manner of the jays also. The jays, perhaps, had a tougher time during the winter than the crows, because they do not eat fish or flesh, but depend mainly upon nuts. A troop of them came eagerly to my ash-heap one morning, which had just been uncovered by the thaw, but they found little except cinders for their gizzards, which, maybe, was what they wanted. They had foraged nearly all winter upon my neighbor's corn-crib, and probably their millstones were dull and needed replacing. They reached the corn through the opening between the slats, and were the envy of the crows, who watched them from the near trees, but dared not venture up. The chickadee, which is an insectivorous bird, will eat corn in winter. It will carry a kernel to the limb of a tree, where, held beneath its tiny foot, it will peck out the eye or chit of the corn, — the germinal part only. I have also seen the woodpecker in winter eat the berries of the poison ivy. Quails will eat the fruit of the poison sumac, and grouse are killed with their crops distended with the leaves of the laurel. Grouse also eat the berries of the bitter-sweet.

The general belief among country people that the jay hoards up nuts for winter use has probably some foundation in fact, though one is at a loss to know where he could place his stores so that they would not be pilfered by the mice and the squirrels. An old hunter told me he had seen jays secreting beechnuts in a knothole in a tree. Probably a red squirrel saw them, too, and laughed behind his tail. One day, in October, two friends of mine, out hunting, saw a blue jay carrying off chestnuts to a spruce swamp. He came and went with great secrecy and dispatch. He had several hundred yards to fly each way, but occupied only a few minutes each trip. The hunters lay in wait to shoot him, but so quickly would he seize his chestnut and be off, that he made more than a dozen trips before they killed him.

A lady writing to me from Iowa says: "I must tell you what I saw a blue jay do last winter. Flying down to the ground in front of the house, he put something in the dead grass, drawing the grass over it, first on one side, then on the other, tramped it down just exactly as a squirrel would, then walked around the spot, examining it to see if it was satisfactory. After he had flown away, I went out to see what he had hidden; it was a nicely shucked peanut that he had laid up for a time of scarcity." Since then I have myself made similar observations. I have several times seen jays carry off chestnuts and hide them here and there upon the ground. They put only one in a place, and covered it up with grass or leaves. Instead, therefore, of hoarding up nuts for future use, when the jay carries them off, he is really planting them. When the snows come these nuts are lost to him, even if he remembered the hundreds of places where he had dropped them. May not this fact account in a measure for the oak and chestnut trees that spring up where a pine forest has been cleared from the ground? Probably the crows secrete nuts in the same way. The acorns at least germinate and remain small, insignificant shoots until the pine is cut away and they have a chance. In almost any pine wood these baby oaks may be seen scattered here and there. Jays will carry off and secrete corn in the same way. One winter I put out ears of corn near my study window to attract these birds. They were not long in finding them out, nor long in stripping the cob of its kernels. They finally came to the window-sill and picked up the loose kernels I scattered there. At no time did they eat any on the spot, but were solely intent on carrying it away. They would take eight or ten grains at a time, apparently holding it in the throat and bill. They carried it away and deposited it in all manner of places; sometimes on the ground, sometimes in decayed trees. Once I saw a jay deposit his load in an old worm's nest in a near-by apple-tree. Whether these stores were visited afterward by the birds, I cannot say. Red-headed woodpeckers have been seen to fill crevices in posts and rails with acorns, where they were found and eaten by gray squirrels. Oregon and Mexican woodpeckers drill holes in decayed trees, and store them with acorns, putting but one acorn in a hole, but hundreds of holes in a tree or branch.

A bevy of quail in my vicinity got through the winter by feeding upon the little black beans contained in the pods of the common locust. For many weeks their diet must have been almost entirely leguminous. The surface snow in the locust-grove which they frequented was crossed in every direction with their fine tracks, like a chain-stitch upon muslins, showing where they went from pod to pod and extracted the contents. Where quite a large branch, filled with pods, lay upon the snow, it looked as if the whole flock had dined or breakfasted off it. The wind seemed to shake down the pods about as fast as they were needed. When a fresh fall of snow had blotted out everything, it was not many hours before the wind had placed upon the cloth another course; but it was always the same old course — beans, beans. What would the birds and the fowls do during such winters, if the trees and the shrubs and the plants all dropped their fruit and their seeds in the fall, as they do their leaves? They would nearly all perish. The apples that cling to the trees, the pods that hang to the lowest branches, and the seeds that the various weeds and grasses hold above the deepest snows, alone make it possible for many birds to pass the winter among us. The red squirrel, too, what would he do? He lays up no stores like the provident chipmunk, but scours about for food in all weathers, feeding upon the seeds in the cones of the hemlock that still cling to the tree, upon sumac-bobs, and the seeds of frozen apples. I have seen the ground under a wild apple-tree that stood near the woods completely covered with the "chonkings" of the frozen apples, the work of the squirrels in getting at the seeds; not an apple had been left, and apparently not a seed had been lost. But the squirrels in this particular locality evidently got pretty hard up before spring, for they developed a new source of food-supply. A young bushy-topped sugar-maple, about forty feet high, standing beside a stone fence near the woods, was attacked, and more than half denuded of its bark. The object of the squirrels seemed to be to get at the soft, white, mucilaginous substance (cambium layer), between the bark and the wood. The ground was covered with fragments of the bark, and the white, naked stems and branches had been scraped by fine teeth. When the sap starts in the early spring, the squirrels add this to their scanty supplies. They perforate the bark of the branches of the maples with their chisel-like teeth, and suck the sweet liquid as it slowly oozes out. It is not much as food, but evidently it helps.

I have said the red squirrel does not lay by a store of food for winter use, like the chipmunk and the wood-mice; yet in the fall he sometimes hoards in a tentative, temporary kind of way. I have seen his savings — butternuts and black walnuts — stuck

here and there in saplings and trees near his nest;
sometimes carefully inserted in the upright fork of
a limb or twig. One day, late in November, I
counted a dozen or more black walnuts put away in
this manner in a little grove of locusts, chestnuts,
and maples by the roadside, and could but smile
at the wise forethought of the rascally squirrel.
His supplies were probably safer that way than if
more elaborately hidden. They were well distributed; his eggs were not all in one basket, and he
could go away from home without any fear that his
storehouse would be broken into in his absence.
The next week, when I passed that way, the nuts
were all gone but two. I saw the squirrel that
doubtless laid claim to them, on each occasion.

There is one thing the red squirrel knows unerringly that I do not (there are probably several
other things); that is, on which side of the butternut the meat lies. He always gnaws through the
shell so as to strike the kernel broadside, and thus
easily extract it; while to my eyes there is no
external mark or indication, in the form or appearance of the nut, as there is in the hickory nut, by
which I can tell whether the edge or the side of the
meat is toward me. But examine any number of
nuts that the squirrels have rifled, and, as a rule,
you will find they always drill through the shell at
the one spot where the meat will be most exposed.
It stands them in hand to know, and they do know.

HARD FARE

Doubtless, if butternuts were a main source of my food, and I were compelled to gnaw into them, I, too, should learn on which side my bread was buttered.

A hard winter affects the chipmunks very little; they are snug and warm in their burrows in the ground and under the rocks, with a bountiful store of nuts or grain. I have heard of nearly a half-bushel of chestnuts being taken from a single den. They usually hole in November, and do not come out again till March or April, unless the winter is very open and mild. Gray squirrels, when they have been partly domesticated in parks and groves near dwellings, are said to hide their nuts here and there upon the ground, and in winter to dig them up from beneath the snow, always hitting the spot accurately. A pair of flying squirrels which I observed one season in an unoccupied country-house had a pile of large, fine chestnuts near their nest till spring, when the nuts disappeared. They probably kept them till the period of greatest scarcity, and until their young made demands upon them.

The woodpeckers and chickadees doubtless find food as plentiful during severe winters as during more open ones, because they confine their search almost entirely to the trunks and branches of trees, where the latter pick up the eggs of insects and various microscopic titbits, and where the former find their accustomed fare of eggs and larvæ also.

An enamel of ice upon the trees alone puts an embargo upon their supplies. At such seasons the ruffed grouse "buds" or goes hungry; while the snowbirds, snow buntings, Canada sparrows, goldfinches, shore larks, and redpolls are dependent upon the weeds and grasses that rise above the snow, and upon the litter of the haystack and barnyard. Neither do the deep snows and the severe cold materially affect the supplies of the rabbit. The deeper the snow, the nearer he is brought to the tops of the tender bushes and shoots. I see in my walks where he has cropped the tops of the small, bushy, soft maples, cutting them slantingly as you would do with a knife, and quite as smoothly. Indeed, the mark was so like that of a knife that, notwithstanding the tracks, it was only after the closest scrutiny that I was convinced it was the sharp, chisel-like teeth of the rabbit. He leaves no chips, and apparently makes clean work of every twig he cuts off.

The wild or native mice usually lay up stores in the fall, in the shape of various nuts, grain, and seeds, yet the provident instinct, as in the red squirrel and in the jay, seems only partly developed in them; instead of carrying these supplies home, they hide them in the nearest convenient place. I have known them to carry a pint or more of hickory nuts and deposit them in a pair of boots standing in the chamber of an outhouse. Near the chestnut-trees they will fill little pocket-like depressions in the ground with chestnuts ; in a grain-field they carry the grain under stones ; under some cover beneath cherry-trees they collect great numbers of cherry-pits. Hence, when cold weather comes, instead of staying at home like the chipmunk, they gad about hither and thither looking up their supplies. One may see their tracks on the snow everywhere in the woods and fields and by the roadside. The advantage of this way of living is that it leads to activity, and probably to sociability.

These wild mice are fond of bees and of honey, and they apparently like nothing better than to be allowed to take up their quarters in winter in some vacant space in a hive of bees. A chamber just over the bees seems to be preferred, as here they get the benefit of the warmth generated by the insects. One very cold winter I wrapped up one of my hives with my shawl. Before long I noticed that the shawl was beginning to have a very torn and tattered appearance. On examination, I found that a native mouse had established itself in the top of the hive, and had levied a ruinous tax upon the shawl to make itself a nest. Never was a fabric more completely reduced to its original elements than were large sections of that shawl. It was a masterly piece of analysis. The work of the wheel and the loom was exactly reversed, and what was once shawl was now the finest and softest of wool. The white-footed mouse is much more common along the fences and in the woods than one would suspect. One winter day I set a mouse-trap — the kind known as the delusion trap — beneath some ledges in the edge of the woods, to determine what species of mouse was most active at this season. The snow fell so deeply that I did not visit my trap for two or three weeks. When I did so, it was literally packed full of white-footed mice. There were seven in all, and not room for another. Our woods are full of these little creatures, and they appear to have a happy, social time of it, even in the severest winters. Their little tunnels under the snow and their hurried strides upon its surface may be noted everywhere. They link tree and stump, or rock and tree, by their pretty trails. They evidently travel for adventure and to hear the news, as well as for food. They know that foxes and owls are about, and they keep pretty close to cover. When they cross an exposed place, they do it hurriedly.

Such a winter as I have referred to probably destroys a great many of our half-migratory birds. The mortality appears to be the greatest in the Border States, where so many species, such as sparrows, robins, bluebirds, meadowlarks, kinglets, usually pass the cold season. A great many birds are said to have died in New Jersey and Pennsyl-

vania, including game-birds. A man in Chester
County saw a fox digging in the snow; on examining the spot, he found half a dozen quails frozen
to death. Game-birds and nearly all other birds
will stand the severest weather if food is plenty;
but to hunger and cold both, the hardiest species
may succumb.

Meadowlarks often pass the winter as far north
as Pennsylvania. A man residing in that State
relates how, in the height of the severest cold, three
half-famished larks came to his door in quest of
food. He removed the snow from a small space,
and spread the poor birds a lunch of various grains
and seeds. They ate heartily, and returned again
the next day, and the next, each time bringing one
or more drooping and half-starved companions with
them, till there was quite a flock of them. Their
deportment changed, their forms became erect and
their plumage glossy, and the feeble mendicants became strong and vivacious birds again. These larks
fell in good hands, but I am persuaded that this
species suffered more than any other of our birds
during that winter. In the spring they were unusually late in making their appearance, — the first one
noted by me on the 9th of April, — and they were
scarce in my locality during the whole season.

Birds not of a feather flock together in winter
Hard times or a common misfortune makes all the
world akin. A Noah's ark with antagonistic species

living in harmony is not an improbable circumstance in a forty-day and a forty-night rain. In severe weather, when the snow lies deep on the ground, I frequently see a loose, heterogeneous troop of birds pass my door, engaged in the common search for food: snowbirds, Canada sparrows, and goldfinches on the ground, and kinglets and nuthatches in the tree above, — all drifting slowly in the same direction, — the snowbirds and sparrows closely associated, but the goldfinches rather clannish and exclusive, while the kinglets and nuthatches keep still more aloof. These birds are probably not drawn together, even thus loosely, by any social instincts, but by a common want; all are hungry, and the activity of one species attracts and draws after it another and another. " I will look that way, too," the kinglet and creeper probably said, when they saw the other birds busy, and heard their merry voices.

IV

THE TRAGEDIES OF THE NESTS

THE life of the birds, especially of our migratory song-birds, is a series of adventures and of hairbreadth escapes by flood and field. Very few of them probably die a natural death, or even live out half their appointed days. The home instinct is strong in birds, as it is in most creatures; and I am convinced that every spring a large number of those which have survived the southern campaign return to their old haunts to breed. A Connecticut farmer took me out under his porch one April day, and showed me a phœbe-bird's nest six stories high. The same bird had no doubt returned year after year; and as there was room for only one nest upon her favorite shelf, she had each season reared a new superstructure upon the old as a foundation. I have heard of a white robin — an albino — that nested several years in succession in the suburbs of a Maryland city. A sparrow with a very marked peculiarity of song I have heard several seasons in my own locality. But the birds do not all live to return to their old haunts: the bobolinks and starlings run a gauntlet of fire from the Hudson to

the Savannah, and the robins and meadowlarks and
other song-birds are shot by boys and pot-hunters
in great numbers, — to say nothing of their danger
from hawks and owls. But of those that do return,
what perils beset their nests, even in the most favored localities! The cabins of the early settlers,
when the country was swarming with hostile Indians, were not surrounded by such dangers. The
tender households of the birds are not only exposed
to hostile Indians in the shape of cats and collectors, but to numerous murderous and bloodthirsty
animals, against whom they have no defense but
concealment. They lead the darkest kind of pioneer life, even in our gardens and orchards, and
under the walls of our houses. Not a day or a night
passes, from the time the eggs are laid till the young
are flown, when the chances are not greatly in favor
of the nest being rifled and its contents devoured,
— by owls, skunks, minks, and coons at night, and
by crows, jays, squirrels, weasels, snakes, and rats
during the day. Infancy, we say, is hedged about
by many perils; but the infancy of birds is cradled
and pillowed in peril. An old Michigan settler told
me that the first six children that were born to him
died; malaria and teething invariably carried them
off when they had reached a certain age; but other
children were born, the country improved, and by
and by the babies weathered the critical period, and
the next six lived and grew up. The birds, too,

would no doubt persevere six times and twice six times, if the season were long enough, and finally rear their family, but the waning summer cuts them short, and but few species have the heart and strength to make even the third trial.

The first nest-builders in spring, like the first settlers near hostile tribes, suffer the most casualties. A large proportion of the nests of April and May are destroyed; their enemies have been many months without eggs, and their appetites are keen for them. It is a time, too, when other food is scarce, and the crows and squirrels are hard put. But the second nests of June, and still more the nests of July and August, are seldom molested. It is rarely that the nest of the goldfinch or the cedar-bird is harried.

My neighborhood on the Hudson is perhaps exceptionally unfavorable as a breeding haunt for birds, owing to the abundance of fish crows and of red squirrels; and the season of which this chapter is mainly a chronicle, the season of 1881, seems to have been a black-letter one even for this place, for at least nine nests out of every ten that I observed during that spring and summer failed of their proper issue. From the first nest I noted, which was that of a bluebird, — built (very imprudently, I thought at the time) in a squirrel-hole in a decayed apple-tree, about the last of April, and which came to naught, even the mother bird, I suspect, perishing by a violent death,—to the last, which was that of a snowbird, observed in August, among the Catskills, deftly concealed in a mossy bank by the side of a road that skirted a wood, where the tall thimble blackberries grew in abundance, and from which the last young one was taken, when it was about half grown, by some nocturnal walker or daylight prowler, some untoward fate seemed hovering about them. It was a season of calamities, of violent deaths, of pillage and massacre, among our feathered neighbors. For the first time I noticed that the orioles were not safe in their strong pendent nests. Three broods were started in the apple-trees, only a few yards from the house, where, for several previous seasons, the birds had nested without molestation ; but this time the young were all destroyed when about half grown. Their chirping and chattering, which was so noticeable one day, suddenly ceased the next. The nests were probably plundered at night, and doubtless by the little red screech owl, which I know is a denizen of these old orchards, living in the deeper cavities of the trees. The owl could alight upon the top of the nest, and easily thrust his murderous claw down into its long pocket and seize the young and draw them forth. The tragedy of one of the nests was heightened, or at least made more palpable, by one of the half-fledged birds, either in its attempt to escape or while in the clutches of the enemy, being caught and entangled in one of the horse-hairs by which the nest was stayed and held to the limb above. There it hung bruised and dead, gibbeted to its own cradle. This nest was the theatre of another little tragedy later in the season. Some time in August a bluebird, indulging its propensity to peep and pry into holes and crevices, alighted upon it and probably inspected the interior ; but by some unlucky move it got its wings entangled in this same fatal horse-hair. Its efforts to free itself appeared only to result in its being more securely and hopelessly bound ; and there it perished ; and there its form, dried and embalmed by the summer heats, was yet hanging in September, the outspread wings and plumage showing nearly as bright as in life.

A correspondent writes me that one of his orioles got entangled in a cord while building her nest, and that, though by the aid of a ladder he reached and liberated her, she died soon afterward. He also found a " chippie" (called also " hair-bird ") suspended from a branch by a horse-hair, beneath a partly constructed nest. I heard of a cedar-bird caught and destroyed in the same way, and of two young bluebirds, around whose legs a horse-hair had become so tightly wound that the legs withered up and dropped off. The birds became fledged, and finally left the nest with the others. Such tragedies are probably quite common.

Before the advent of civilization in this country, the oriole probably built a much deeper nest than it usually does at present. When now it builds in remote trees and along the borders of the woods, its nest, I have noticed, is long and gourd-shaped ; but in orchards and near dwellings it is only a deep cup or pouch. It shortens it up in proportion as the danger lessens. Probably a succession of disastrous years, like the one under review, would cause it to lengthen it again beyond the reach of owl's talons or jay-bird's beak.

The first song sparrow's nest I observed in the spring of 1881 was in a field under a fragment of a board, the board being raised from the ground a couple of inches by two poles. It had its full complement of eggs, and probably sent forth a brood of young birds, though as to this I cannot speak positively, as I neglected to observe it further. It was well sheltered and concealed, and was not easily come at by any of its natural enemies, save snakes and weasels. But concealment often avails little. In May, a song sparrow, which had evidently met with disaster earlier in the season, built its nest in a thick mass of woodbine against the side of my house, about fifteen feet from the ground. Perhaps it took the hint from its cousin, the English sparrow. The nest was admirably placed, protected from the storms by the overhanging eaves and from all eyes by the thick screen of leaves. Only by patiently watching the suspicious bird, as she lingered near with food in her beak, did I discover its whereabouts. That brood is safe, I thought, beyond doubt. But it was not: the nest was pillaged one night, either by an owl, or else by a rat that had climbed into the vine, seeking an entrance to the house. The mother bird, after reflecting upon her ill-luck about a week, seemed to resolve to try a different system of tactics, and to throw all appearances of concealment aside. She built a nest a few yards from the house, beside the drive, upon a smooth piece of greensward. There was not a weed or a shrub or anything whatever to conceal it or mark its site. The structure was completed, and incubation had begun, before I discovered what was going on. "Well, well," I said, looking down upon the bird almost at my feet, "this is going to the other extreme indeed ; now the cats will have you." The desperate little bird sat there day after day, looking like a brown leaf pressed down in the short green grass. As the weather grew hot, her position became very trying. It was no longer a question of keeping the eggs warm, but of keeping them from roasting. The sun had no mercy on her, and she fairly panted in the middle of the day. In such an emergency the male robin has been known to perch above the sitting female and shade her with his outstretched wings. But in this case there was no perch for the male bird, had he been

disposed to make a sunshade of himself. I thought
to lend a hand in this direction myself, and so
stuck a leafy twig beside the nest. This was probably an unwise interference: it guided disaster to
the spot ; the nest was broken up, and the mother
bird was probably caught, as I never saw her afterward.

For several previous summers a pair of kingbirds
had reared, unmolested, a brood of young in an
apple-tree, only a few yards from the house; but
during this season disaster overtook them also.
The nest was completed, the eggs laid, and incubation had just begun, when, one morning about
sunrise, I heard loud cries of distress and alarm
proceed from the old apple-tree. Looking out
of the window, I saw a crow, which I knew to be
a fish crow, perched upon the edge of the nest, hastily bolting the eggs. The parent birds, usually so
ready for the attack, seemed overcome with grief
and alarm. They fluttered about in the most helpless and bewildered manner, and it was not till the
robber fled on my approach that they recovered
themselves and charged upon him. The crow scur-
ried away with upturned, threatening head, the
furious kingbirds fairly upon his back. The pair
lingered around their desecrated nest for several
days, almost silent, and saddened by their loss, and
then disappeared. They probably made another
trial elsewhere.

THE TRAGEDIES OF THE NESTS

The fish crow fishes only when it has destroyed all the eggs and young birds it can find. It is the most despicable thief and robber among our feathered creatures. From May to August it is gorged with the fledgelings of the nest. It is fortunate that its range is so limited. In size it is smaller than the common crow, and it is a much less noble and dignified bird. Its caw is weak and feminine, — a sort of split and abortive caw, that stamps it the sneak-thief it is. This crow is common farther south, but is not found in this State, so far as I have observed, except in the valley of the Hudson.

One season a pair of them built a nest in a Norway spruce that stood amid a dense growth of other ornamental trees near a large unoccupied house. They sat down amid plenty. The wolf established himself in the fold. The many birds — robins, thrushes, finches, vireos, pewees — that seek the vicinity of dwellings (especially of these large country residences with their many trees and park-like grounds), for the greater safety of their eggs and young, were the easy and convenient victims of these robbers. They plundered right and left, and were not disturbed till their young were nearly fledged, when some boys, who had long before marked them as their prize, rifled the nest.

The song-birds nearly all build low; their cradle is not upon the treetop. It is only birds of prey that fear danger from below more than from above,

75

and that seek the higher branches for their nests.
A line five feet from the ground would run above
more than half the nests, and one ten feet would
bound more than three fourths of them. It is only
the oriole, the wood pewee, the tanager, the war-
bling vireo, and two or three warblers, that, as a
rule, go higher than this. The crows and jays and
other enemies of the birds have learned to explore
this belt pretty thoroughly. But the leaves and
the protective coloring of most nests baffle them as
effectually, no doubt, as they do the professional
oölogist. The nest of the red-eyed vireo is one of
the most artfully placed in the wood. It is just
beyond the point where the eye naturally pauses
in its search; namely, on the extreme end of the
lowest branch of the tree, usually four or five feet
from the ground. One looks up and down and
through the tree, — shoots his eye-beams into it as
he might discharge his gun at some game hidden
there, but the drooping tip of that low horizontal
branch, — who would think of pointing his piece
just there? If a crow or other marauder were to
alight upon the branch or upon those above it, the
nest would be screened from him by the large leaf
that usually forms a canopy immediately above it.
The nest-hunter, standing at the foot of the tree
and looking straight before him, might discover it
easily, were it not for its soft, neutral gray tint
which blends so thoroughly with the trunks and

branches of trees. Indeed, I think there is no nest in the woods — no arboreal nest — so well concealed. The last one I saw was pendent from the end of a low branch of a maple, that nearly grazed the clapboards of an unused hay-barn in a remote backwoods clearing. I peeped through a crack, and saw the old birds feed the nearly fledged young within a few inches of my face. And yet the cowbird finds this nest and drops her parasitical egg in it. Her tactics in this as in other cases are probably to watch the movements of the parent bird. She may often be seen searching anxiously through the trees or bushes for a suitable nest, yet she may still oftener be seen perched upon some good point of observation watching the birds as they come and go about her. There is no doubt that, in many cases, the cowbird makes room for her own illegitimate egg in the nest by removing one of the bird's own. When the cowbird finds two or more eggs in a nest in which she wishes to deposit her own, she will remove one of them. I found a sparrow's nest with two sparrow's eggs and one cowbird's egg, and another egg lying a foot or so below it on the ground. I replaced the ejected egg, and the next day found it again removed, and another cowbird's egg in its place. I put it back the second time, when it was again ejected, or destroyed, for I failed to find it anywhere. Very alert and sensitive birds, like the warblers, often bury the strange egg beneath a second nest built on top of the old. A lady living in the suburbs of an eastern city, one morning heard cries of distress from a pair of house wrens that had a nest in a honeysuckle on her front porch. On looking out of the window, she beheld this little comedy, — comedy from her point of view, but no doubt grim tragedy from the point of view of the wrens: a cowbird with a wren's egg in its beak running rapidly along the walk, with the outraged wrens forming a procession behind it, screaming, scolding, and gesticulating as only these voluble little birds can. The cowbird had probably been surprised in the act of violating the nest, and the wrens were giving her a piece of their minds.

Every cowbird is reared at the expense of two or more song-birds. For every one of these dusky little pedestrians there amid the grazing cattle there are two or more sparrows, or vireos, or warblers, the less. It is a big price to pay, — two larks for a bunting, — two sovereigns for a shilling; but Nature does not hesitate occasionally to contradict herself in just this way. The young of the cowbird is disproportionately large and aggressive, one might say hoggish. When disturbed, it will clasp the nest and scream and snap its beak threateningly. One hatched out in a song sparrow's nest which was under my observation, and would soon have overridden and overborne the young sparrow which

78

came out of the shell a few hours later, had I not interfered from time to time and lent the young sparrow a helping hand. Every day I would visit the nest and take the sparrow out from under the pot-bellied interloper, and place it on top, so that presently it was able to hold its own against its enemy. Both birds became fledged and left the nest about the same time. Whether the race was an even one after that, I know not.

I noted but two warblers' nests during that season, one of the black-throated blue-back and one of the redstart, — the latter built in an apple-tree but a few yards from a little rustic summer-house where I idle away many summer days. The lively little birds, darting and flashing about, attracted my attention for a week before I discovered their nest. They probably built it by working early in the morning, before I appeared upon the scene, as I never saw them with material in their beaks. Guessing from their movements that the nest was in a large maple that stood near by, I climbed the tree and explored it thoroughly, looking especially in the forks of the branches, as the authorities say these birds build in a fork. But no nest could I find. Indeed, how can one by searching find a bird's-nest? I overshot the mark; the nest was much nearer me, almost under my very nose, and I discovered it, not by searching, but by a casual glance of the eye, while thinking of other matters.

The bird was just settling upon it as I looked up from my book and caught her in the act. The nest was built near the end of a long, knotty, horizontal branch of an apple-tree, but effectually hidden by the grouping of the leaves; it had three eggs, one of which proved to be barren. The two young birds grew apace, and were out of the nest early in the second week; but something caught one of them the first night. The other probably grew to maturity, as it disappeared from the vicinity with its parents after some days.

The blue-back's nest was scarcely a foot from the ground, in a little bush situated in a low, dense wood of hemlock and beech and maple amid the Catskills, — a deep, massive, elaborate structure, in which the sitting bird sank till her beak and tail alone were visible above the brim. It was a misty chilly day when I chanced to find the nest, and the mother bird knew instinctively that it was not prudent to leave her four half-incubated eggs uncovered and exposed for a moment. When I sat down near the nest, she grew very uneasy, and, after trying in vain to decoy me away by suddenly dropping from the branches and dragging herself over the ground as if mortally wounded, she approached and timidly and half doubtingly covered her eggs within two yards of where I sat. I disturbed her several times, to note her ways. There came to be something almost appealing in her looks and manner, and she would keep her place on her precious eggs till my outstretched hand was within a few feet of her. Finally, I covered the cavity of the nest with a dry leaf. This she did not remove with her beak, but thrust her head deftly beneath it and shook it off upon the ground. Many of her sympathizing neighbors, attracted by her alarm note, came and had a peep at the intruder, and then flew away, but the male bird did not appear upon the scene. The final history of this nest I am unable to give, as I did not again visit it till late in the season, when, of course, it was empty.

Years pass without my finding a brown thrasher's nest; it is not a nest you are likely to stumble upon in your walk; it is hidden as a miser hides his gold, and watched as jealously. The male pours out his rich and triumphant song from the tallest tree he can find, and fairly challenges you to come and look for his treasures in his vicinity. But you will not find them if you go. The nest is somewhere on the outer circle of his song; he is never so imprudent as to take up his stand very near it. The artists who draw those cozy little pictures of a brooding mother bird, with the male perched but a yard away in full song, do not copy from nature. The thrasher's nest I found was thirty or forty rods from the point where the male was wont to indulge in his brilliant recitative. It was in an open field under a low ground-juniper. My dog disturbed the sitting bird as I was passing near. The nest could be seen only by lifting up and parting away the branches. All the arts of concealment had been carefully studied. It was the last place you would think of looking, and, if you did look, nothing was visible but the dense green circle of the low-spreading juniper. When you approached, the bird would keep her place till you had begun to stir the branches, when she would start out, and, just skimming the ground, make a bright brown line to the near fence and bushes. I confidently expected that this nest would escape molestation, but it did not. Its discovery by myself and dog probably opened the door for ill-luck, as one day, not long afterward, when I peeped in upon it, it was empty. The proud song of the male had ceased from his accustomed tree, and the pair were seen no more in that vicinity.

The phœbe-bird is a wise architect, and perhaps enjoys as great an immunity from danger, both in its person and its nest, as any other bird. Its modest, ashen-gray suit is the color of the rocks where it builds, and the moss of which it makes such free use gives to its nest the look of a natural growth or accretion. But when it comes into the barn or under the shed to build, as it so frequently does, the moss is rather out of place. Doubtless in time the bird will take the hint, and when she builds in such places will leave the moss out. I

noted but two nests the summer I am speaking of:
one in a barn failed of issue, on account of the rats,
I suspect, though the little owl may have been the
depredator ; the other, in the woods, sent forth
three young. This latter nest was most charmingly
and ingeniously placed. I discovered it while in
quest of pond-lilies, in a long, deep, level stretch of
water in the woods. A large tree had blown over
at the edge of the water, and its dense mass of upturned roots, with the black, peaty soil filling the
interstices, was like the fragment of a wall several
feet high, rising from the edge of the languid current. In a niche in this earthy wall, and visible
and accessible only from the water, a phœbe had
built her nest and reared her brood. I paddled
my boat up and came alongside prepared to take
the family aboard. The young, nearly ready to
fly, were quite undisturbed by my presence, having probably been assured that no danger need be
apprehended from that side. It was not a likely
place for minks, or they would not have been so
secure.

I noted but one nest of the wood pewee, and that,
too, like so many other nests, failed of issue. It was
saddled upon a small dry limb of a plane-tree that
stood by the roadside, about forty feet from the
ground. Every day for nearly a week, as I passed
by, I saw the sitting bird upon the nest. Then one
morning she was not in her place, and on examina-

tion the nest proved to be empty, — robbed, I had no doubt, by the red squirrels, as they were very abundant in its vicinity, and appeared to make a clean sweep of every nest. The wood pewee builds an exquisite nest, shaped and finished as if cast in a mould. It is modeled without and within with equal neatness and art, like the nest of the hummingbird and the little gray gnatcatcher. The material is much more refractory than that used by either of these birds, being, in the present case, dry, fine cedar twigs; but these were bound into a shape as rounded and compact as could be moulded out of the most plastic material. Indeed, the nest of this bird looks precisely like a large, lichen-covered, cup-shaped excrescence of the limb upon which it is placed. And the bird, while sitting, seems entirely at her ease. Most birds seem to make very hard work of incubation. It is a kind of martyrdom which appears to tax all their powers of endurance. They have such a fixed, rigid, predetermined look, pressed down into the nest and as motionless as if made of cast-iron. But the wood pewee is an exception. She is largely visible above the rim of the nest. Her attitude is easy and graceful; she moves her head this way and that, and seems to take note of whatever goes on about her; and if her neighbor were to drop in for a little social chat, she could doubtless do her part. In fact, she makes light and easy work of what, to most other birds, is such a serious and engrossing matter. If it does not look like play with her, it at least looks like leisure and quiet contemplation.

There is no nest-builder that suffers more from crows and squirrels and other enemies than the wood thrush. It builds as openly and unsuspiciously as if it thought all the world as honest as itself. Its favorite place is the fork of a sapling, eight or ten feet from the ground, where it falls an easy prey to every nest-robber that comes prowling through the woods and groves. It is not a bird that skulks and hides, like the catbird, the brown thrasher, the chat, or the chewink, and its nest is not concealed with the same art as theirs. Our thrushes are all frank, open-mannered birds; but the veery and the hermit build upon the ground, where they at least escape the crows, owls, and jays, and stand a better chance to be overlooked by the red squirrel and weasel also; while the robin seeks the protection of dwellings and outbuildings. For years I have not known the nest of a wood thrush to succeed. During the season referred to I observed but two, both apparently a second attempt, as the season was well advanced, and both failures. In one case, the nest was placed in a branch that an apple-tree, standing near a dwelling, held out over the highway. The structure was barely ten feet above the middle of the road, and would just escape a passing load of hay. It was made conspicuous by the use of a large fragment of newspaper in its foundation, — an unsafe material to build upon in most cases. Whatever else the press may guard, this particular newspaper did not guard this nest from harm. It saw the egg and probably the chick, but not the fledgeling. A murderous deed was committed above the public highway, but whether in the open day or under cover of darkness I have no means of knowing. The frisky red squirrel was doubtless the culprit. The other nest was in a maple sapling, within a few yards of the little rustic summer-house already referred to. The first attempt of the season, I suspect, had failed in a more secluded place under the hill; so the pair had come up nearer the house for protection. The male sang in the trees near by for several days before I chanced to see the nest. The very morning, I think, it was finished, I saw a red squirrel exploring a tree but a few yards away; he probably knew what the singing meant as well as I did. I did not see the inside of the nest, for it was almost instantly deserted, the female having probably laid a single egg, which the squirrel had devoured.

If I were a bird, in building my nest I should follow the example of the bobolink, placing it in the midst of a broad meadow, where there was no spear of grass, or flower, or growth unlike another to mark its site. I judge that the bobolink escapes the dangers to which I have adverted as few or no other birds do. Unless the mowers come along at an earlier date than she has anticipated, that is, before July 1, or a skunk goes nosing through the grass, which is unusual, she is as safe as bird well can be in the great open of nature. She selects the most monotonous and uniform place she can find amid the daisies or the timothy and clover, and places her simple structure upon the ground in the midst of it. There is no concealment, except as the great conceals the little, as the desert conceals the pebble, as the myriad conceals the unit. You may find the nest once, if your course chances to lead you across it, and your eye is quick enough to note the silent brown bird as she darts swiftly away; but step three paces in the wrong direction, and your search will probably be fruitless. My friend and I found a nest by accident one day, and then lost it again one minute afterward. I moved away a few yards to be sure of the mother bird, charging my friend not to stir from his tracks. When I returned, he had moved two paces, he said (he had really moved four), and we spent a half hour stooping over the daisies and the buttercups, looking for the lost clew. We grew desperate, and fairly felt the ground over with our hands, but without avail. I marked the spot with a bush, and came the next day, and, with the bush as a centre, moved about it in slowly increasing circles, covering, I thought, nearly every inch of ground with my feet, and laying hold of it with all the visual power I could command, till my patience was exhausted, and I gave up, baffled. I began to doubt the ability of the parent birds themselves to find it, and so secreted myself and watched. After much delay, the male bird appeared with food in his beak, and, satisfying himself that the coast was clear, dropped into the grass which I had trodden down in my search. Fastening my eye upon a particular meadow-lily, I walked straight to the spot, bent down, and gazed long and intently into the grass. Finally my eye separated the nest and its young from its surroundings. My foot had barely missed them in my search, but by how much they had escaped my eye I could not tell. Probably not by distance at all, but simply by unrecognition. They were virtually invisible. The dark gray and yellowish brown dry grass and stubble of the meadow-bottom were exactly copied in the color of the half-fledged young. More than that, they hugged the nest so closely and formed such a compact mass, that though there were five of them, they preserved the unit of expression, — no single head or form was defined; they were one, and that one was without shape or color, and not separable, except by closest scrutiny, from the one of the meadow-bottom. That nest prospered, as bobolinks' nests doubtless generally do; for, notwithstanding the enormous slaughter of the birds during their fall migrations by Southern sportsmen, the bobolink appears to hold its own, and its music does not diminish in our Northern meadows.

Birds with whom the struggle for life is the sharpest seem to be more prolific than those whose nest and young are exposed to fewer dangers. The robin, the sparrow, the pewee, will rear, or make the attempt to rear, two and sometimes three broods in a season; but the bobolink, the oriole, the kingbird, the goldfinch, the cedar-bird, the birds of prey, and the woodpeckers, that build in safe retreats in the trunks of trees, have usually but a single brood. If the bobolink reared two broods, our meadows would swarm with them.

I noted three nests of the cedar-bird in August in a single orchard, all productive, but each with one or more unfruitful eggs in it. The cedar-bird is the most silent of our birds, having but a single fine note, so far as I have observed, but its manners are very expressive at times. No bird known to me is capable of expressing so much silent alarm while on the nest as this bird. As you ascend the tree and draw near it, it depresses its plumage and crest, stretches up its neck, and becomes the very picture of fear. Other birds, under like circumstances, hardly change their expression at all till they launch into the air, when by their voice they express anger rather than alarm.

I have referred to the red squirrel as a destroyer of the eggs and young of birds. I think the mischief it does in this respect can hardly be overestimated. Nearly all birds look upon it as their enemy, and attack and annoy it when it appears near their breeding haunts. Thus, I have seen the pewee, the cuckoo, the robin, and the wood thrush pursuing it with angry voice and gestures. A friend of mine saw a pair of robins attack one in the top of a tall tree so vigorously that they caused it to lose its hold, when it fell to the ground, and was so stunned by the blow as to allow him to pick it up. If you wish the birds to breed and thrive in your orchards and groves, kill every red squirrel that infests the place; kill every weasel also. The weasel is a subtle and arch enemy of the birds. It climbs trees and explores them with great ease and nimbleness. I have seen it do so on several occasions. One day my attention was arrested by the angry notes of a pair of brown thrashers that were flitting from bush to bush along an old stone row in a remote field. Presently I saw what it was that excited them, — three large red weasels, or ermines, coming along the stone wall, and leisurely and half playfully exploring every tree that stood near it. They had probably robbed the thrashers. They would go up the trees with great ease, and glide serpent-like out upon the main branches. When they descended the tree, they were unable to come straight down, like a squirrel, but went around it spirally. How boldly they thrust their heads out of the wall, and eyed me and sniffed me as I drew near, — their round, thin ears, their prominent, glistening, bead-like eyes, and the curving, snake-like motions of the head and neck being very noticeable. They looked like blood-suckers and egg-suckers. They suggested something extremely remorseless and cruel. One could understand the alarm of the rats when they discover one of these fearless, subtle, and circumventing creatures threading their holes. To flee must be like trying to escape death itself. I was one day standing in the woods upon a flat stone, in what at certain seasons was the bed of a stream, when one of these weasels came undulating along and ran under the stone upon which I was standing. As I remained motionless, he thrust out his wedge-shaped head, and turned it back above the stone as if half in mind to seize my foot; then he drew back, and presently went his way. These weasels often hunt in packs like the British stoat. When I was a boy, my father one day armed me with an old musket and sent me to shoot chipmunks around the corn. While watching the squirrels, a troop of weasels tried to cross a barway where I sat, and were so bent on doing it that I fired at them, boy-like, simply to thwart their purpose. One of the weasels was disabled by my shot, but the troop were not discouraged, and, after making several feints to cross, one of them seized the wounded one and bore it over, and the pack disappeared in the wall on the other side.

Let me conclude this chapter with two or three more notes about this alert enemy of the birds and the lesser animals, the weasel.

A farmer one day heard a queer growling sound in the grass ; on approaching the spot he saw two weasels contending over a mouse ; both had hold of the mouse, pulling in opposite directions, and they were so absorbed in the struggle that the farmer cautiously put his hands down and grabbed them both by the back of the neck. He put them in a cage, and offered them bread and other food. This they refused to eat, but in a few days one of them had eaten the other up, picking his bones clean, and leaving nothing but the skeleton.

The same farmer was one day in his cellar when two rats came out of a hole near him in great haste, and ran up the cellar wall and along its top till they came to a floor timber that stopped their progress, when they turned at bay, and looked excitedly back along the course they had come. In a moment a weasel, evidently in hot pursuit of them, came out of the hole, and, seeing the farmer, checked his course and darted back. The rats had doubtless turned to give him fight, and would probably have been a match for him.

The weasel seems to track its game by scent. A hunter of my acquaintance was one day sitting in the woods, when he saw a red squirrel run with great speed up a tree near him, and out upon a long branch, from which he leaped to some rocks, and disappeared beneath them. In a moment a weasel came in full course upon his trail, ran up the tree, then out along the branch, from the end of which he leaped to the rocks as the squirrel did, and plunged beneath them.

Doubtless the squirrel fell a prey to him. The squirrel's best game would have been to have kept to the higher treetops, where he could easily have distanced the weasel. But beneath the rocks he stood a very poor chance. I have often wondered what keeps such an animal as the weasel in check, for weasels are quite rare. They never need go hungry, for rats and squirrels and mice and birds are everywhere. They probably do not fall a prey to any other animal, and very rarely to man. But the circumstances or agencies that check the increase of any species of animal or bird are, as Darwin says, very obscure and but little known.

V

A SNOW–STORM

THAT is a striking line with which Emerson opens his beautiful poem of the Snow-Storm:

> " Announced by all the trumpets of the sky,
>   Arrives the snow, and, driving o'er the fields,
>   Seems nowhere to alight."

One seems to see the clouds puffing their cheeks as they sound the charge of their white legions. But the line is more accurately descriptive of a rain-storm, as, in both summer and winter, rain is usually preceded by wind. Homer, describing a snow-storm in his time, says : —

> " The winds are lulled."

The preparations of a snow-storm are, as a rule, gentle and quiet ; a marked hush pervades both the earth and the sky. The movements of the celestial forces are muffled, as if the snow already paved the way of their coming. There is no uproar, no clashing of arms, no blowing of wind trumpets. These soft, feathery, exquisite crystals are formed as if in the silence and privacy of the inner cloud-chambers. Rude winds would break the spell and mar the process. The clouds are smoother, and slower in their movements, with less definite outlines than those which bring rain. In fact, everything is prophetic of the gentle and noiseless meteor that is approaching, and of the stillness that is to succeed it, when " all the batteries of sound are spiked," as Lowell says, and "we see the movements of life as a deaf man sees it, — a mere wraith of the clamorous existence that inflicts itself on our ears when the ground is bare." After the storm is fairly launched the winds not infrequently awake, and, seeing their opportunity, pipe the flakes a lively dance.. I am speaking now of the typical, full-born midwinter storm that comes to us from the north or north-northeast, and that piles the landscape knee-deep with snow. Such a storm once came to us the last day of January, — the master-storm of the winter. Previous to that date, we had had but light snow. The spruces had been able to catch it all upon their arms, and keep a circle of bare ground beneath them where the birds scratched. But the day following this fall, they stood with their lower branches completely buried. If the Old Man of the North had but sent us his couriers and errand-boys before, the old graybeard appeared himself at our doors on this occasion, and we were all his subjects. His flag was upon every tree and roof, his seal upon every door and window, and his embargo upon every path

and highway. He slipped down upon us, too, under
the cover of such a bright, seraphic day, — a day
that disarmed suspicion with all but the wise ones,
a day without a cloud or a film, with a gentle breeze
from the west, a dry, bracing air, a blazing sun that
brought out the bare ground under the lee of the
fences and farm-buildings, and at night a spotless
moon near her full. The next morning the sky red-
dened in the east, then became gray, heavy, and silent. A seamless cloud covered it. The smoke from
the chimneys went up with a barely perceptible slant
toward the north. In the forenoon the cedar-birds,
purple finches, yellowbirds, nuthatches, bluebirds,
were in flocks or in couples and trios about the trees,
more or less noisy and loquacious. About noon a
thin white veil began to blur the distant southern
mountains. It was like a white dream slowly de-
scending upon them. The first flake or flakelet that
reached me was a mere white speck that came idly
circling and eddying to the ground. I could not see
it after it alighted. It might have been a scale from
the feather of some passing bird, or a larger mote in
the air that the stillness was allowing to settle. Yet
it was the altogether inaudible and infinitesimal
trumpeter that announced the coming storm, the
grain of sand that heralded the desert. Presently
another fell, then another ; the white mist was
creeping up the river valley. How slowly and loiter-
ingly it came, and how microscopic its first siftings !

This mill is bolting its flour very fine, you think. But wait a little ; it gets coarser by and by ; you begin to see the flakes ; they increase in numbers and in size, and before one o'clock it is snowing steadily. The flakes come straight down, but in a half hour they have a marked slant toward the north ; the wind is taking a hand in the game. By mid-afternoon the storm is coming in regular pulse-beats or in vertical waves. The wind is not strong, but seems steady ; the pines hum, yet there is a sort of rhythmic throb in the meteor ; the air toward the wind looks ribbed with steady-moving vertical waves of snow. The impulses travel along like undulations in a vast suspended white curtain, imparted by some invisible hand there in the northeast. As the day declines the storm waxes, the wind increases, the snow-fall thickens, and

> " the housemates sit
> Around the radiant fireplace, inclosed
> In a tumultuous privacy of storm,"

a privacy which you feel outside as well as in. Out of doors you seem in a vast tent of snow ; the distance is shut out, near-by objects are hidden ; there are white curtains above you, and white screens about you, and you feel housed and secluded in storm. Your friend leaves your door, and he is wrapped away in white obscurity, caught up in a cloud, and his footsteps are obliterated. Travelers

98

meet on the road, and do not see or hear each other
till they are face to face. The passing train, half a
mile away, gives forth a mere wraith of sound. Its
whistle is deadened as in a dense wood.

Still the storm rose. At five o'clock I went forth
to face it in a two-mile walk. It was exhilarating in
the extreme. The snow was lighter than chaff. It
had been dried in the Arctic ovens to the last degree. The foot sped through it without hindrance.
I fancied the grouse and the quail quietly sitting
down in the open places, and letting it drift over
them. With head under wing, and wing snugly
folded, they would be softly and tenderly buried in
a few moments. The mice and the squirrels were
in their dens, but I fancied the fox asleep upon some
rock or log, and allowing the flakes to cover him.
The hare in her form, too, was being warmly sepul-
chred with the rest. I thought of the young cattle
and the sheep huddled together on the lee side of
a haystack in some remote field, all enveloped in
mantles of white.

> " I thought me on the ourie cattle,
>   Or silly sheep, wha bide this brattle
>   O' wintry war,
>   Or thro' the drift, deep-lairing sprattle,
>   Beneath a scaur.
>
> " Ilk happing bird, wee helpless thing,
>   That in the merry months o' spring

Delighted me to hear thee sing,
What comes o' thee?
Where wilt thou cow'r thy chittering wing,
And close thy ee?"

As I passed the creek, I noticed the white woolly masses that filled the water. It was as if somebody upstream had been washing his sheep and the water had carried away all the wool, and I thought of the Psalmist's phrase, "He giveth snow like wool." On the river a heavy fall of snow simulates a thin layer of cotton batting. The tide drifts it along, and, where it meets with an obstruction alongshore, it folds up and becomes wrinkled or convoluted like a fabric, or like cotton sheeting. Attempt to row a boat through it, and it seems indeed like cotton or wool, every fibre of which resists your progress.

As the sun went down and darkness fell, the storm impulse reached its full. It became a wild conflagration of wind and snow ; the world was wrapt in frost flame ; it enveloped one, and penetrated his lungs and caught away his breath like a blast from a burning city. How it whipped around and under every cover and searched out every crack and crevice, sifting under the shingles in the attic, darting its white tongue under the kitchen door, puffing its breath down the chimney, roaring through the woods, stalking like a sheeted ghost across the hills, bending in white and ever-changing forms above the fences, sweeping across the plains, whirl-

100

ing in eddies behind the buildings, or leaping spitefully up their walls, — in short, taking the world
entirely to itself, and giving a loose rein to its
desire.

But in the morning, behold! the world was not
consumed ; it was not the besom of destruction,
after all, but the gentle hand of mercy. How
deeply and warmly and spotlessly Earth's nakedness
is clothed! — the "wool" of the Psalmist nearly
two feet deep. And as far as warmth and protection are concerned, there is a good deal of the
virtue of wool in such a snow-fall. How it protects
the grass, the plants, the roots of the trees, and the
worms, insects, and smaller animals in the ground!
It is a veritable fleece, beneath which the shivering
earth ("the frozen hills ached with pain," says one
of our young poets) is restored to warmth. When
the temperature of the air is at zero, the thermometer, placed at the surface of the ground beneath a
foot and a half of snow, would probably indicate
but a few degrees below freezing ; the snow is rendered such a perfect non-conductor of heat mainly
by reason of the quantity of air that is caught and
retained between the crystals. Then how, like a
fleece of wool, it rounds and fills out the landscape,
and makes the leanest and most angular field look
smooth!

The day dawned, and continued as innocent and
fair as the day which had preceded, — two moun-

tain peaks of sky and sun, with their valley of cloud and snow between. Walk to the nearest spring run on such a morning, and you can see the Colorado valley and the great cañons of the West in miniature, carved in alabaster. In the midst of the plain of snow lie these chasms; the vertical walls, the bold headlands, the turrets and spires and obelisks, the rounded and towering capes, the carved and buttressed precipices, the branch valleys and cañons, and the winding and tortuous course of the main channel are all here, — all that the Yosemite or the Yellowstone have to show, except the terraces and the cascades. Sometimes my cañon is bridged, and my fancy runs nimbly across a vast arch of Parian marble, and that makes up for the falls and the terraces. Where the ground is marshy, I come upon a pretty and vivid illustration of what I have read and been told of the Florida formation. This white and brittle limestone is undermined by water. Here are the dimples and depressions, the sinks and the wells, the springs and the lakes. Some places a mouse might break through the surface and reveal the water far beneath, or the snow gives way of its own weight, and you have a minute Florida well, with the truncated cone-shape and all. The arched and subterranean pools and passages are there likewise.

But there is a more beautiful and fundamental geology than this in the snow-storm: we are ad-

mitted into Nature's oldest laboratory, and see the
working of the law by which the foundations of the
material universe were laid, — the law or mystery
of crystallization. The earth is built upon crystals;
the granite rock is only a denser and more compact
snow, or a kind of ice that was vapor once and may
be vapor again. "Every stone is nothing else but
a congealed lump of frozen earth," says Plutarch.
By cold and pressure air can be liquefied, perhaps
solidified. A little more time, a little more heat,
and the hills are but April snow-banks. Nature has
but two forms, the cell and the crystal, — the crystal first, the cell last. All organic nature is built up
of the cell; all inorganic, of the crystal. Cell upon
cell rises the vegetable, rises the animal; crystal
wedded to and compacted with crystal stretches
the earth beneath them. See in the falling snow
the old cooling and precipitation, and the shooting,
radiating forms that are the architects of planet and
globe.

We love the sight of the brown and ruddy earth;
it is the color of life, while a snow-covered plain is
the face of death; yet snow is but the mask of the
life-giving rain; it, too, is the friend of man, — the
tender, sculpturesque, immaculate, warming, fertilizing snow.

VI

A TASTE OF MAINE BIRCH

THE traveler and camper-out in Maine, unless he penetrates its more northern portions, has less reason to remember it as a pine-tree State than a birch-tree State. The white-pine forests have melted away like snow in the spring and gone down-stream, leaving only patches here and there in the more remote and inaccessible parts. The portion of the State I saw — the valley of the Kennebec and the woods about Moxie Lake — had been shorn of its pine timber more than forty years before, and is now covered with a thick growth of spruce and cedar and various deciduous trees. But the birch abounds. Indeed, when the pine goes out the birch comes in; the race of men succeeds the race of giants. This tree has great stay-at-home virtues. Let the sombre, aspiring, mysterious pine go; the birch has humble, every-day uses. In Maine, the paper or canoe birch is turned to more account than any other tree. I read in Gibbon that the natives of ancient Assyria used to celebrate in verse or prose the three hundred and sixty uses to which the various parts and products of the palm-tree were

105

applied. The Maine birch is turned to so many accounts that it may well be called the palm of this region. Uncle Nathan, our guide, said it was made especially for the camper-out ; yes, and for the woodman and frontiersman generally. It is a magazine, a furnishing store set up in the wilderness, whose goods are free to every comer. The whole equipment of the camp lies folded in it, and comes forth at the beck of the woodman's axe: tent, waterproof roof, boat, camp utensils, buckets, cups, plates, spoons, napkins, table-cloths, paper for letters or your journal, torches, candles, kindling-wood, and fuel. The canoe birch yields you its vestments with the utmost liberality. Ask for its coat, and it gives you its waistcoat also. Its bark seems wrapped about it layer upon layer, and comes off with great ease. We saw many rude structures and cabins shingled and sided with it, and haystacks capped with it. Near a maple-sugar camp there was a large pile of birch-bark sap-buckets, — each bucket made of a piece of bark about a yard square, folded up as the tinman folds up a sheet of tin to make a square vessel, the corners bent around against the sides and held by a wooden pin. When, one day, we were overtaken by a shower in traveling through the woods, our guide quickly stripped large sheets of the bark from a near tree, and we had each a perfect umbrella as by magic. When the rain was over, and we moved on, I wrapped mine about me

106

A TASTE OF MAINE BIRCH

like a large leather apron, and it shielded my clothes
from the wet bushes. When we came to a spring,
Uncle Nathan would have a birch-bark cup ready
before any of us could get a tin one out of his knap-
sack, and I think water never tasted so sweet as
from one of these bark cups. It is exactly the
thing. It just fits the mouth, and it seems to give
new virtues to the water. It makes me thirsty now
when I think of it. In our camp at Moxie, we
made a large birch-bark box to keep the butter
in; and the butter in this box, covered with some
leafy boughs, I think improved in flavor day by
day. Maine butter needs something to mollify
and sweeten it a little, and I think birch bark will
do it. In camp Uncle Nathan often drank his tea
and coffee from a bark cup; the china closet in
the birch-tree was always handy, and our vulgar
tinware was generally a good deal mixed, and the
kitchen maid not at all particular about dish-wash-
ing. We all tried the oatmeal with the maple syrup
in one of these dishes, and the stewed mountain
cranberries, using a birch-bark spoon, and never
found service better. Uncle Nathan declared he
could boil potatoes in a bark kettle, and I did not
doubt him. Instead of sending our soiled napkins
and table-spreads to the wash, we rolled them up
into candles and torches, and drew daily upon our
stores in the forest for new ones.

But the great triumph of the birch is, of course,

the bark canoe. When Uncle Nathan took us out
under his little woodshed, and showed us, or rather
modestly permitted us to see, his nearly finished
canoe, it was like a first glimpse of some new and
unknown genius of the woods or streams. It sat
there on the chips and shavings and fragments of
bark like some shy, delicate creature just emerged
from its hiding-place, or like some wild flower just
opened. It was the first boat of the kind I had
ever seen, and it filled my eye completely. What
woodcraft it indicated, and what a wild, free life,
sylvan life, it promised! It had such a fresh, aboriginal look as I had never before seen in any
kind of handiwork. Its clear, yellow-red color would
have become the cheek of an Indian maiden. Then
its supple curves and swells, its sinewy stays and
thwarts, its bow-like contour, its tomahawk stem
and stern rising quickly and sharply from its frame,
were all vividly suggestive of the race from which
it came. An old Indian had taught Uncle Nathan
the art, and the soul of the ideal red man looked
out of the boat before us. Uncle Nathan had spent
two days ranging the mountains looking for a suitable tree, and had worked nearly a week on the
craft. It was twelve feet long, and would seat and
carry five men nicely. Three trees contribute to
the making of a canoe, beside the birch, namely,
the white cedar for ribs and lining, the spruce for
roots and fibres to sew its joints and bind its frame,

and the pine for pitch or rosin to stop its seams
and cracks. It is hand-made and home-made, or
rather wood-made, in a sense that no other craft
is, except a dugout, and it suggests a taste and a
refinement that few products of civilization realize.
The design of a savage, it yet looks like the thought
of a poet, and its grace and fitness haunt the imagination. I suppose its production was the inevitable result of the Indian's wants and surroundings,
but that does not detract from its beauty. It is,
indeed, one of the fairest flowers the thorny plant
of necessity ever bore. Our canoe, as I have inti-
mated, was not yet finished when we first saw it, nor
yet when we took it up, with its architect, upon our
metaphorical backs and bore it to the woods. It
lacked part of its cedar lining and the rosin upon its
joints, and these were added after we reached our
destination.

Though we were not indebted to the birch-tree
for our guide, Uncle Nathan, as he was known in
all that country, yet he matched well these woodsy
products and conveniences. The birch-tree had
given him a large part of his tuition, and, kneeling
in his canoe and making it shoot noiselessly over
the water with that subtle yet indescribably expressive and athletic play of the muscles of the back
and shoulders, the boat and the man seemed born
of the same spirit. He had been a hunter and
trapper for over forty years ; he had grown gray in

the woods, had ripened and matured there, and
everything about him was as if the spirit of the
woods had had the ordering of it; his whole
make-up was in a minor and subdued key, like
the moss and the lichens, or like the protective
coloring of the game, — everything but his quick
sense and penetrative glance. He was as gentle and
modest as a girl; his sensibilities were like plants
that grow in the shade. The woods and the solitudes
had touched him with their own softening and refining influence; had, indeed, shed upon his soil of
life a rich, deep leaf mould that was delightful, and
that nursed, half concealed, the tenderest and wildest growths. There was grit enough back of and
beneath it all, but he presented none of the rough
and repelling traits of character of the conventional
backwoodsman. In the spring he was a driver of
logs on the Kennebec, usually having charge of a
large gang of men; in the winter he was a solitary
trapper and hunter in the forests.

Our first glimpse of Maine waters was Pleasant
Pond, which we found by following a white, rapid,
musical stream from the Kennebec three miles back
into the mountains. Maine waters are for the most
part dark-complexioned, Indian-colored streams,
but Pleasant Pond is a pale-face among them both
in name and nature. It is the only strictly silver
lake I ever saw. Its waters seem almost artificially
white and brilliant, though of remarkable transpar-

ency. I think I detected minute shining motes held
in suspension in it. As for the trout, they are veritable bars of silver until you have cut their flesh, when
they are the reddest of gold. They have no crimson or other spots, and the straight lateral line is
but a faint pencil-mark. They appeared to be a
species of lake trout peculiar to these waters, uniformly from ten to twelve inches in length. And
these beautiful fish, at the time of our visit (last
of August) at least, were to be taken only in deep
water upon a hook baited with salt pork. And
then you needed a letter of introduction to them.
They were not to be tempted or cajoled by stran-
gers. We did not succeed in raising a fish, although
instructed how it was to be done, until one of the
natives, a young and obliging farmer living hard
by, came and lent his countenance to the enterprise. I sat in one end of the boat and he in the
other, my pork was the same as his, and I manœu-
vred it as directed, and yet those fish knew his hook
from mine in sixty feet of water, and preferred it
four times in five. Evidently they did not bite because they were hungry, but solely for old acquaintance' sake.

Pleasant Pond is an irregular sheet of water, two
miles or more in its greatest diameter, with high
rugged mountains rising up from its western shore,
and low rolling hills sweeping back from its eastern
and northern, covered by a few sterile farms. I

was never tired, when the wind was still, of floating along its margin and gazing down into its marvelously translucent depths. The boulders and fragments of rocks were seen, at a depth of twenty-five or thirty feet, strewing its floor, and apparently as free from any covering of sediment as when they were dropped there by the old glaciers æons ago. Our camp was amid a dense grove of second growth of white pine on the eastern shore, where, for one, I found a most admirable cradle in a little depression outside of the tent, carpeted with pine needles, in which to pass the night. The camper-out is always in luck if he can find, sheltered by the trees, a soft hole in the ground, even if he has a stone for a pillow. The earth must open its arms a little for us even in life, if we are to sleep well upon its bosom. I have often heard my grandfather, who was a soldier of the Revolution, tell with great gusto how he once bivouacked in a little hollow made by the overturning of a tree, and slept so soundly that he did not wake up till his cradle was half full of water from a passing shower.

What bird or other creature might represent the divinity of Pleasant Pond I do not know, but its demon, as of most northern inland waters, is the loon; and a very good demon he is, too, suggesting something not so much malevolent as arch, sardonic, ubiquitous, circumventing, with just a tinge of something inhuman and uncanny. His fiery-red

eyes gleaming forth from that jet-black head are
full of meaning. Then his strange horse-laughter
by day, and his weird, doleful cry at night, like that
of a lost and wandering spirit, recall no other bird or
beast. He suggests something almost supernatural
in his alertness and amazing quickness, cheating
the shot and the bullet of the sportsman out of
their aim. I know of but one other bird so quick,
and that is the hummingbird, which I never have
been able to kill with a gun. The loon laughs the
shotgun to scorn, and the obliging young farmer
above referred to told me he had shot at them
hundreds of times with his rifle, without effect, —
they always dodged his bullet. We had in our
party a breech-loading rifle, which weapon is perhaps an appreciable moment of time quicker than
the ordinary muzzle-loader, and this the poor loon
could not or did not dodge. He had not timed
himself to that species of firearms, and when, with
his fellow, he swam about within rifle range of our
camp, letting off volleys of his wild, ironical *ha-ha*,
he little suspected the dangerous gun that was
matched against him. As the rifle cracked, both
loons made the gesture of diving, but only one of
them disappeared beneath the water; and when he
came to the surface in a few moments, a hundred
or more yards away, and saw his companion did
not follow, but was floating on the water where he
had last seen him, he took the alarm and sped away

in the distance. The bird I had killed was a magnificent specimen, and I looked him over with great interest. His glossy checkered coat, his banded neck, his snow-white breast, his powerful lance-shaped beak, his red eyes, his black, thin, slender, marvelously delicate feet and legs, issuing from his muscular thighs, and looking as if they had never touched the ground, his strong wings well forward, while his legs were quite at the apex, and the neat, elegant model of the entire bird, speed and quickness and strength stamped upon every feature, — all delighted and lingered in the eye. The loon appears like anything but a silly bird, unless you see him in some collection, or in the shop of the taxidermist, where he usually looks very tame and goose-like. Nature never meant the loon to stand up, or to use his feet and legs for other purposes than swimming. Indeed, he cannot stand except upon his tail in a perpendicular attitude; but in the collections he is poised upon his feet like a barn-yard fowl, all the wildness and grace and alertness gone out of him. My specimen sits upon a table as upon the surface of the water, his feet trailing behind him, his body low and trim, his head elevated and slightly turned as if in the act of bringing that fiery eye to bear upon you, and vigilance and power stamped upon every lineament.

The loon is to the fishes what the hawk is to the birds ; he swoops down to unknown depths upon

them, and not even the wary trout can elude him.
Uncle Nathan said he had seen the loon disappear,
and in a moment come up with a large trout, which
he would cut in two with his strong beak and
swallow piecemeal. Neither the loon nor the otter
can bolt a fish under the water; he must come to
the surface to dispose of it. (I once saw a man eat
a cake under water in London.) Our guide told
me he had seen the parent loon swimming with a
single young one upon its back. When closely
pressed, it dived, or "div," as he would have it,
and left the young bird sitting upon the water.
Then it too disappeared, and when the old one
returned and called, it came out from the shore.
On the wing overhead the loon looks not unlike
a very large duck, but when it alights, it plows
into the water like a bombshell. It probably cannot take flight from the land, as the one Gilbert
White saw and describes in his letters was picked
up in a field, unable to launch itself into the air.

From Pleasant Pond we went seven miles through
the woods to Moxie Lake, following an overgrown
lumberman's "tote" road, our canoe and supplies
hauled on a sled by the young farmer with his
three-year-old steers. I doubt if birch-bark ever
made a rougher voyage than that. As I watched it
above the bushes, the sled and the luggage being
hidden, it appeared as if tossed in the wildest and
most tempestuous sea. When the bushes closed

above it, I felt as if it had gone down, or been broken into a hundred pieces. Billows of rocks and logs, and chasms of creeks and spring runs, kept it rearing and pitching in the most frightful manner. The steers went at a spanking pace; indeed, it was a regular bovine gale; but their driver clung to their side amid the brush and boulders with desperate tenacity, and seemed to manage them by signs and nudges, for he hardly uttered his orders aloud. But we got through without any serious mishap, passing Mosquito Creek and Mosquito Pond, and flanking Mosquito Mountain, but seeing no mosquitoes, and brought up at dusk at a lumberman's old hay-barn, standing in the midst of a lonely clearing on the shores of Moxie Lake.

Here we passed the night, and were lucky in having a good roof over our heads, for it rained heavily. After we were rolled in our blankets and variously disposed upon the haymow, Uncle Nathan lulled us to sleep by a long and characteristic yarn.

I had asked him, half jocosely, if he believed in "spooks;" but he took my question seriously, and without answering it directly, proceeded to tell us what he himself had known and witnessed. It was, by the way, extremely difficult either to surprise or to steal upon any of Uncle Nathan's private opinions and beliefs about matters and things. He was as shy of all debatable subjects as a fox is of a trap. He usually talked in a circle, just as he

116

hunted moose and caribou, so as not to approach
his point too rudely and suddenly. He would keep
on the lee side of his interlocutor in spite of all one
could do. He was thoroughly good and reliable,
but the wild creatures of the woods, in pursuit of
which he had spent so much of his life, had taught
him a curious gentleness and indirection, and to
keep himself in the background; he was careful
that you should not scent his opinions upon any
subject at all polemic, but he would tell you what
he had seen and known. What he had seen and
known about spooks was briefly this : In company
with a neighbor he was passing the night with an
old recluse who lived somewhere in these woods.
Their host was an Englishman, who had the repu-
tation of having murdered his wife some years before in another part of the country, and, deserted by
his grown-up children, was eking out his days in
poverty amid these solitudes. The three men were
sleeping upon the floor, with Uncle Nathan next to
a rude partition that divided the cabin into two
rooms. At his head there was a door that opened
into this other apartment. Late at night, Uncle
Nathan said, he awoke and turned over, and his
mind was occupied with various things, when he
heard somebody behind the partition. He reached
over and felt that both of his companions were in
their places beside him, and he was somewhat surprised. The person, or whatever it was, in the other

room moved about heavily, and pulled the table from its place beside the wall to the middle of the floor. "I was not dreaming," said Uncle Nathan; "I felt of my eyes twice to make sure, and they were wide open." Presently the door opened; he was sensible of the draught upon his head, and a woman's form stepped heavily past him; he felt the "swirl" of her skirts as she went by. Then there was a loud noise in the room, as if some one had fallen his whole length upon the floor. "It jarred the house," said he, "and woke everybody up. I asked old Mr. —— if he heard that noise. 'Yes,' said he, 'it was thunder.' But it was not thunder, I know that;" and then added, "I was no more afraid than I am this minute. I never was the least mite afraid in my life. And my eyes were wide open," he repeated; "I felt of them twice; but whether that was the speret of that man's murdered wife or not, I cannot tell. They said she was an uncommon heavy woman." Uncle Nathan was a man of unusually quick and acute senses, and he did not doubt their evidence on this occasion any more than he did when they prompted him to level his rifle at a bear or a moose.

Moxie Lake lies much lower than Pleasant Pond, and its waters compared with those of the latter are as copper compared with silver. It is very irregular in shape; now narrowing to the dimensions of a slow-moving grassy creek, then expanding into a broad deep basin with rocky shores, and commanding the noblest mountain scenery. It is rarely that the pond-lily and the speckled trout are found together, — the fish the soul of the purest spring water, the flower the transfigured spirit of the dark mud and slime of sluggish summer streams and ponds ; yet in Moxie they were both found in perfection. Our camp was amid the birches, poplars, and white cedars near the head of the lake, where the best fishing at this season was to be had. Moxie has a small oval head, rather shallow, but bumpy with rocks ; a long, deep neck, full of springs, where the trout lie ; and a very broad chest, with two islands tufted with pine-trees for breasts. We swam in the head, we fished in the neck, or in a small section of it, a space about the size of the Adam's apple, and we paddled across and around the broad expanse below. Our birch-bark was not finished and christened till we reached Moxie. The cedar lining was completed at Pleasant Pond, where we had the use of a *bateau*, but the rosin was not applied to the seams till we reached this lake. When I knelt down in it for the first time, and put its slender maple paddle into the water, it sprang away with such quickness and speed that it disturbed me in my seat. I had spurred a more restive and spirited steed than I was used to. In fact, I had never been in a craft that sustained so close a relation to my will, and was so responsive to my slightest wish. When I caught my first large trout from it, it sympathized a little too closely, and my enthusiasm started a leak, which, however, with a live coal and a piece of rosin, was quickly mended. You cannot perform much of a war-dance in a birch-bark canoe; better wait till you get on dry land. Yet as a boat it is not so shy and "ticklish" as I had imagined. One needs to be on the alert, as becomes a sportsman and an angler, and in his dealings with it must charge himself with three things, — precision, moderation, and circumspection.

Trout weighing four and five pounds have been taken at Moxie, but none of that size came to our hand. I realized the fondest hopes I had dared to indulge in when I hooked the first two-pounder of my life, and my extreme solicitude lest he get away I trust was pardonable. My friend, in relating the episode in camp, said I had implored him to row me down in the middle of the lake that I might have room to manœuvre my fish. But the slander has barely a grain of truth in it. The water near us showed several old stakes broken off just below the surface, and my fish was determined to wrap my leader about one of these stakes; it was only for the clear space a few yards farther out that I prayed. It was not long after that my friend found himself in an anxious frame of mind. He hooked a large trout, which came home on him so suddenly

that he had not time to reel up his line, and in
his extremity he stretched his tall form into the air
and lifted up his pole to an incredible height. He
checked the trout before it got under the boat, but
dared not come down an inch, and then began his
amusing further elongation in reaching for his reel
with one hand, while he carried it ten feet into the
air with the other. A step-ladder would perhaps
have been more welcome to him just then than at
any other moment during his life. But the trout was
saved, though my friend's buttons and suspenders
suffered.

We learned a new trick in fly-fishing here, worth
disclosing. It was not one day in four that the
trout would take the fly on the surface. When
the south wind was blowing and the clouds threat-
ened rain, they would at times, notably about three
o'clock, rise handsomely. But on all other occasions it was rarely that we could entice them up
through the twelve or fifteen feet of water. Earlier
in the season they are not so lazy and indifferent,
but the August languor and drowsiness were now
upon them. So we learned by a lucky accident
to fish deep for them, even weighting our leaders
with a shot, and allowing the flies to sink nearly
to the bottom. After a moment's pause we would
draw them slowly up, and when half or two thirds
of the way to the top the trout would strike, when
the sport became lively enough. Most of our fish

were taken in this way. There is nothing like the
flash and the strike at the surface, and perhaps
only the need of food will ever tempt the genuine
angler into any more prosaic style of fishing; but if
you must go below the surface, a shotted leader is
the best thing to use.

Our camp-fire at night served more purposes than
one; from its embers and flickering shadows, Uncle
Nathan read us many a tale of his life in the woods.
They were the same old hunter's stories, except
that they evidently had the merit of being strictly
true, and hence were not very thrilling or marvel-
ous. Uncle Nathan's tendency was rather to tone
down and belittle his experiences than to exagger-
ate them. If he ever bragged at all (and I suspect
he did just a little, when telling us how he outshot
one of the famous riflemen of the American team,
whom he was guiding through these woods), he did
it in such a sly, roundabout way that it was hard
to catch him at it. His passage with the rifleman
referred to shows the difference between the prac-
tical offhand skill of the hunter in the woods and
the science of the long-range target-hitter. Mr.
Bull's Eye had heard that his guide was a capital
shot, and had seen some proof of it, and hence could
not rest till he had had a trial of skill with him.
Uncle Nathan, being the challenged party, had the
right to name the distance and the conditions. A
piece of white paper the size of a silver dollar was

put up on a tree twelve rods off, the contestants to fire three shots each offhand. Uncle Nathan's first bullet barely missed the mark, but the other two were planted well into it. Then the great rifleman took his turn, and missed every time.

"By hemp!" said Uncle Nathan, "I was sorry I shot so well, Mr. —— took it so to heart ; and I had used his own rifle, too. He did not get over it for a week."

But far more ignominious was the failure of Mr. Bull's Eye when he saw his first bear. They were paddling slowly and silently down Dead River, when the guide heard a slight noise in the bushes just behind a little bend. He whispered to the rifleman, who sat kneeling in the bow of the boat, to take his rifle. But instead of doing so, he picked up his two-barreled shotgun. As they turned the point, there stood a bear not twenty yards away, drinking from the stream. Uncle Nathan held the canoe, while the man who had come so far in quest of this very game was trying to lay down his shotgun and pick up his rifle. " His hand moved like the hand of a clock," said Uncle Nathan, "and I could hardly keep my seat. I knew the bear would see us in a moment more and run." Instead of laying his gun by his side, where it belonged, he reached it across in front of him, and laid it upon his rifle, and in trying to get the latter from under it a noise was made; the bear heard it and raised his head. Still there was time, for as the bear sprang into the woods he stopped and looked back, — " as I knew he would," said the guide; yet the marksman was not ready. " By hemp! I could have shot three bears," exclaimed Uncle Nathan, " while he was getting that rifle to his face!"

Poor Mr. Bull's Eye was deeply humiliated. " Just the chance I had been looking for," he said, " and my wits suddenly left me."

As a hunter, Uncle Nathan always took the game on its own terms, that of still-hunting. He even shot foxes in this way, going into the fields in the fall just at break of day, and watching for them about their mousing haunts. One morning, by these tactics, he shot a black fox; a fine specimen, he said, and a wild one, for he stopped and looked and listened every few yards.

He had killed over two hundred moose, a large number of them at night on the lakes. His method was to go out in his canoe and conceal himself by some point or island, and wait till he heard the game. In the fall the moose comes into the water to eat the large fibrous roots of the pond-lilies. He splashes along till he finds a suitable spot, when he begins feeding, sometimes thrusting his head and neck several feet under water. The hunter listens, and when the moose lifts his head and the rills of water run from it, and he hears him " swash " the lily roots about to get off the mud, it is his time to start. Silently as a shadow he creeps up on the moose, who, by the way, it seems, never suspects the approach of danger from the water side. If the hunter accidentally makes a noise, the moose looks toward the shore for it. There is always a slight gleam on the water, Uncle Nathan says, even in the darkest night, and the dusky form of the moose can be distinctly seen upon it. When the hunter sees this darker shadow, he lifts his gun to the sky and gets the range of its barrels, then lowers it till it covers the mark, and fires.

The largest moose Uncle Nathan ever killed is mounted in the State House at Augusta. He shot him while hunting in winter on snow-shoes. The moose was reposing upon the ground, with his head stretched out in front of him, as one may sometimes see a cow resting. The position was such that only a quartering shot through the animal's hip could reach its heart. Studying the problem carefully, and taking his own time, the hunter fired. The moose sprang into the air, turned, and came with tremendous strides straight toward him. "I knew he had not seen or scented me," said Uncle Nathan, "but, by hemp, I wished myself somewhere else just then; for I was lying right down in his path." But the noble animal stopped a few yards short, and fell dead with a bullet hole through his heart.

When the moose yard in the winter, that is,

restrict their wanderings to a well-defined section
of the forest or mountain, trampling down the snow
and beating paths in all directions, they browse off
only the most dainty morsels first; when they go
over the ground a second time they crop a little
cleaner; the third time they sort still closer, till
by and by nothing is left. Spruce, hemlock, pop-
lar, the barks of various trees, everything within
reach, is cropped close. When the hunter comes
upon one of these yards, the problem for him to
settle is, Where are the moose? for it is absolutely
necessary that he keep on the lee side of them.
So he considers the lay of the land, the direction of
the wind, the time of day, the depth of the snow,
examines the spoor, the cropped twigs, and studies
every hint and clew like a detective. Uncle Nathan
said he could not explain to another how he did it,
but he could usually tell in a few minutes in what
direction to look for the game. His experience
had ripened into a kind of intuition or winged
reasoning that was above rules.

He said that most large game, — deer, caribou,
moose, bear, — when started by the hunter and not
much scared, were sure to stop and look back before
disappearing from sight; he usually waited for this
last and best chance to fire. He told us of a huge
bear he had seen one morning while still-hunting
foxes in the fields; the bear saw him, and got into
the woods before he could get a good shot. In her

126

course, some distance up the mountain, was a bald, open spot, and he felt sure when she crossed this spot she would pause and look behind her ; and sure enough, like Lot's wife, her curiosity got the better of her; she stopped to have a final look, and her travels ended there and then.

Uncle Nathan had trapped and shot a great many bears, and some of his experiences revealed an unusual degree of sagacity in this animal. One April, when the weather began to get warm and thawy, an old bear left her den in the rocks, and built a large, warm nest of grass, leaves, and the bark of the white cedar, under a tall balsam fir that stood in a low, sunny, open place amid the mountains. Hither she conducted her two cubs, and the family began life in what might be called their spring residence. The tree above them was for shelter, and for refuge for the cubs in case danger approached, as it soon did in the form of Uncle Nathan. He happened that way soon after the bear had moved. Seeing her track in the snow, he concluded to follow it. When the bear had passed, the snow had been soft and sposhy, and she had "slumped," he said, several inches. It was now hard and slippery. As he neared the tree, the track turned and doubled, and tacked this way and that, and led through the worst brush and brambles to be found. This was a shrewd thought of the old bear; she could thus hear her enemy coming a long time before he drew very near. When Uncle Nathan finally reached the nest, he found it empty, but still warm. Then he began to circle about and look for the bear's footprints or nailprints upon the frozen snow. Not finding them the first time, he took a larger circle, then a still larger ; finally he made a long detour, and spent nearly an hour searching for some clew to the direction the bear had taken, but all to no purpose. Then he returned to the tree and scrutinized it. The foliage was very dense, but presently he made out one of the cubs near the top, standing up amid the branches, and peering down at him. This he killed. Further search revealed only a mass of foliage apparently more dense than usual, but a bullet sent into it was followed by loud whimpering and crying, and the other baby bear came tumbling down. In leaving the place, greatly puzzled as to what had become of the mother bear, Uncle Nathan followed another of her frozen tracks, and after about a quarter of a mile saw beside it, upon the snow, the fresh trail he had been in search of. In making her escape, the bear had stepped exactly in her old tracks that were hard and icy, and had thus left no mark till she took to the snow again.

During his trapping expeditions into the woods in midwinter, I was curious to know how Uncle Nathan passed the nights, as we were twice pinched with the cold at that season in our tent and blankets. It was no trouble to keep warm, he said, in the coldest weather. As night approached, he would select a place for his camp on the side of a hill. With one of his snow-shoes he would shovel out the snow till the ground was reached, carrying the snow out in front, as we scrape the earth out of the side of a hill to level up a place for the house and yard. On this level place, which, however, was made to incline slightly toward the hill, his bed of boughs was made. On the ground he had uncovered he built his fire. His bed was thus on a level with the fire, and the heat could not thaw the snow under him and let him down, or the burning logs roll upon him. With a steep ascent behind it, the fire burned better, and the wind was not so apt to drive the smoke and blaze in upon him. Then, with the long, curving branches of the spruce stuck thickly around three sides of the bed, and curving over and uniting their tops above it, a shelter was formed that would keep out the cold and the snow, and that would catch and retain the warmth of the fire. Rolled in his blanket in such a nest, Uncle Nathan had passed hundreds of the most frigid winter nights.

One day we made an excursion of three miles through the woods to Bald Mountain, following a dim trail. We saw, as we filed silently along, plenty of signs of caribou, deer, and bear, but were not blessed with a sight of either of the animals them-

selves. I noticed that Uncle Nathan, in looking
through the woods, did not hold his head as we did,
but thrust it slightly forward, and peered under the
branches like a deer, or other wild creature.

The summit of Bald Mountain was the most impressive mountain-top I had ever seen, mainly, perhaps, because it was one enormous crown of nearly
naked granite. The rock had that gray, elemental,
eternal look which granite alone has. One seemed
to be face to face with the gods of the fore-world.
Like an atom, like a breath of to-day, we were
suddenly confronted by abysmal geologic time, —
the eternities past and the eternities to come. The
enormous cleavage of the rocks, the appalling cracks
and fissures, the rent boulders, the smitten granite
floors, gave one a new sense of the power of heat
and frost. In one place we noticed several deep
parallel grooves, made by the old glaciers. In the
depressions on the summit there was a hard, black,
peaty-like soil that looked indescribably ancient and
unfamiliar. Out of this mould, which might have
come from the moon or the interplanetary spaces,
were growing mountain cranberries and blueberries
or huckleberries. We were soon so absorbed in
gathering the latter that we were quite oblivious of
the grandeurs about us. It is these blueberries that
attract the bears. In eating them, Uncle Nathan
said, they take the bushes in their mouths, and by
an upward movement strip them clean both of

leaves and berries. We were constantly on the lookout for the bears, but failed to see any. Yet a few
days afterward, when two of our party returned
here and encamped upon the mountain, they saw
five during their stay, but failed to get a good shot.
The rifle was in the wrong place each time. The
man with the shotgun saw an old bear and two
cubs lift themselves from behind a rock and twist
their noses around for his scent, and then shrink
away. They were too far off for his buckshot. I
must not forget the superb view that lay before us,
a wilderness of woods and waters stretching away
to the horizon on every hand. Nearly a dozen lakes
and ponds could be seen, and in a clearer atmosphere the foot of Moosehead Lake would have been
visible. The highest and most striking mountain
to be seen was Mount Bigelow, rising above Dead
River, far to the west, and its two sharp peaks
notching the horizon like enormous saw-teeth. We
walked around and viewed curiously a huge boulder
on the top of the mountain that had been split in
two vertically, and one of the halves moved a few
feet out of its bed. It looked recent and familiar,
but suggested gods instead of men. The force that
moved the rock had plainly come from the north.
I thought of a similar boulder I had seen not long
before on the highest point of the Shawangunk
Mountains, in New York, one side of which is
propped up with a large stone, as wall-builders prop

up a rock to wrap a chain around it. The rock seems poised lightly, and has but a few points of bearing. In this instance, too, the power had come from the north.

The prettiest botanical specimen my trip yielded was a little plant that bears the ugly name of horned bladderwort, and which I found growing in marshy places along the shores of Moxie Lake. It has a slender, naked stem nearly a foot high, crowned by two or more large deep yellow flowers, — flowers the shape of little bonnets or hoods. One almost expected to see tiny faces looking out of them. This illusion is heightened by the horn or spur of the flower, which projects from the hood like a long tapering chin, — some masker's device. Then the cape behind, — what a smart upward curve it has, as if spurned by the fairy shoulders it was meant to cover ! But perhaps the most notable thing about the flower was its fragrance, — the richest and strongest perfume I have ever found in a wild flower. This our botanist, Gray, does not mention, as if one should describe the lark and forget its song. The fragrance suggested that of white clover, but was more rank and spicy.

The woods about Moxie Lake were literally carpeted with linnæa. I had never seen it in such profusion. In early summer, the period of its bloom, what a charming spectacle the mossy floors of these remote woods must present! The flowers are pur-

plc rose-color, nodding and fragrant. Another very
abundant plant in these woods was the *Clintonia
borealis.* Uncle Nathan said it was called "bear's
corn," though he did not know why. The only
noticeable flower by the Maine roadsides at this
season that is not common in other parts of the
country is the harebell. Its bright blue, bell-shaped
corolla shone out from amid the dry grass and
weeds all along the route. It was one of the most
delicate roadside flowers I had ever seen.

The only new bird I saw in Maine was the
pileated woodpecker, or black "log-cock," called by
Uncle Nathan "woodcock." I had never before
seen or heard this bird, and its loud cackle in the
woods about Moxie was a new sound to me. It is
the wildest and largest of our northern woodpeckers, and the rarest. Its voice and the sound
of its hammer are heard only in the depths of the
northern woods. It is about as large as a crow,
and nearly as black.

We stayed a week at Moxie, or until we became
surfeited with its trout, and had killed the last
merganser duck that lingered about our end of the
lake. The trout that had accumulated on our
hands we had kept alive in a large champagne
basket submerged in the lake, and the morning
we broke camp the basket was towed to the shore
and opened ; and after we had feasted our eyes
upon the superb spectacle, every trout — there were

twelve or fifteen, some of them two-pounders—was allowed to swim back into the lake. They went leisurely, in couples and in trios, and were soon kicking up their heels in their old haunts. I expect that the divinity who presides over Moxie will see to it that every one of those trout, doubled in weight, comes to our basket in the future.

VII

WINTER NEIGHBORS

THE country is more of a wilderness, more of
a wild solitude, in the winter than in the summer. The wild comes out. The urban, the cultivated, is hidden or negatived. You hardly know a
good field from a poor, a meadow from a pasture,
a park from a forest. Lines and boundaries are
disregarded ; gates and bar-ways are unclosed ;
man lets go his hold upon the earth ; title-deeds
are deep buried beneath the snow ; the best-kept
grounds relapse to a state of nature ; under the
pressure of the cold, all the wild creatures become
outlaws, and roam abroad beyond their usual
haunts. The partridge comes to the orchard for
buds ; the rabbit comes to the garden and lawn ;
the crows and jays come to the ash-heap and corn-
crib, the snow buntings to the stack and to the
barnyard ; the sparrows pilfer from the domestic
fowls ; the pine grosbeak comes down from the
north and shears your maples of their buds ; the fox
prowls about your premises at night ; and the red
squirrels find your grain in the barn or steal the
butternuts from your attic. In fact, winter, like

some great calamity, changes the status of most
creatures and sets them adrift. Winter, like poverty, makes us acquainted with strange bedfellows.

For my part, my nearest approach to a strange
bedfellow is the little gray rabbit that has taken up
her abode under my study floor. As she spends
the day here and is out larking at night, she is not
much of a bedfellow, after all. It is probable that
I disturb her slumbers more than she does mine. I
think she is some support to me under there, — a
silent, wide-eyed witness and backer; a type of the
gentle and harmless in savage nature. She has
no sagacity to give me or to lend me, but that soft,
nimble foot of hers, and that touch as of cotton
wherever she goes, are worthy of emulation. I
think I can feel her good-will through the floor,
and I hope she can mine. When I have a happy
thought, I imagine her ears twitch, especially when
I think of the sweet apple I will place by her
doorway at night. I wonder if that fox chanced
to catch a glimpse of her the other night when he
stealthily leaped over the fence near by and walked
along between the study and the house? How
clearly one could read that it was not a little dog
that had passed there! There was something furtive in the track; it shied off away from the house
and around it, as if eying it suspiciously; and then
it had the caution and deliberation of the fox, —
bold, bold, but not too bold; wariness was in every

footprint. If it had been a little dog that had
chanced to wander that way, when he crossed my
path he would have followed it up to the barn and
have gone smelling around for a bone; but this
sharp, cautious track held straight across all others,
keeping five or six rods from the house, up the
hill, across the highway toward a neighboring farm-
stead, with its nose in the air, and its eye and ear
alert, so to speak.

A winter neighbor of mine, in whom I am interested, and who perhaps lends me his support
after his kind, is a little red owl, whose retreat is in
the heart of an old apple-tree just over the fence.
Where he keeps himself in spring and summer, I
do not know, but late every fall, and at intervals
all winter, his hiding-place is discovered by the
jays and nuthatches, and proclaimed from the treetops for the space of half an hour or so, with all
the powers of voice they can command. Four times
during one winter they called me out to behold this
little ogre feigning sleep in his den, sometimes in
one apple-tree, sometimes in another. Whenever
I heard their cries, I knew my neighbor was being
berated. The birds would take turns at looking in
upon him, and uttering their alarm-notes. Every
jay within hearing would come to the spot, and
at once approach the hole in the trunk or limb,
and with a kind of breathless eagerness and excitement take a peep at the owl, and then join the

outcry. When I approached they would hastily take a final look, and then withdraw and regard my movements intently. After accustoming my eye to the faint light of the cavity for a few moments, I could usually make out the owl at the bottom feigning sleep. Feigning, I say, because this is what he really did, as I first discovered one day when I cut into his retreat with the axe. The loud blows and the falling chips did not disturb him at all. When I reached in a stick and pulled him over on his side, leaving one of his wings spread out, he made no attempt to recover himself, but lay among the chips and fragments of decayed wood, like a part of themselves. Indeed, it took a sharp eye to distinguish him. Not till I had pulled him forth by one wing, rather rudely, did he abandon his trick of simulated sleep or death. Then, like a detected pickpocket, he was suddenly transformed into another creature. His eyes flew wide open, his talons clutched my finger, his ears were depressed, and every motion and look said, "Hands off, at your peril." Finding this game did not work, he soon began to "play possum" again. I put a cover over my study wood-box and kept him captive for a week. Look in upon him at any time, night or day, and he was apparently wrapped in the profoundest slumber ; but the live mice which I put into his box from time to time found his sleep was easily broken ; there would be a sud-

138

den rustle in the box, a faint squeak, and then silence. After a week of captivity I gave him his freedom in the full sunshine : no trouble for him to see which way and where to go.

Just at dusk in the winter nights, I often hear his soft *bur-r-r-r*, very pleasing and bell-like. What a furtive, woody sound it is in the winter stillness, so unlike the harsh scream of the hawk! But all the ways of the owl are ways of softness and duskiness. His wings are shod with silence, his plumage is edged with down.

Another owl neighbor of mine, with whom I pass the time of day more frequently than with the last, lives farther away. I pass his castle every night on my way to the post-office, and in winter, if the hour is late enough, am pretty sure to see him standing in his doorway, surveying the passers-by and the landscape through narrow slits in his eyes. For four successive winters now have I observed him. As the twilight begins to deepen, he rises up out of his cavity in the apple-tree, scarcely faster than the moon rises from behind the hill, and sits in the opening, completely framed by its outlines of gray bark and dead wood, and by his protective coloring virtually invisible to every eye that does not know he is there. Probably my own is the only eye that has ever penetrated his secret, and mine never would have done so had I not chanced on one occasion to see him leave his retreat and make a raid upon a shrike that was impaling a shrew-mouse upon a thorn in a neighboring tree, and which I was watching. Failing to get the mouse, the owl returned swiftly to his cavity, and ever since, while going that way, I have been on the lookout for him. Dozens of teams and foot-passengers pass him late in the day, but he regards them not, nor they him. When I come along and pause to salute him, he opens his eyes a little wider, and, appearing to recognize me, quickly shrinks and fades into the background of his door in a very weird and curious manner. When he is not at his outlook, or when he is, it requires the best powers of the eye to decide the point, as the empty cavity itself is almost an exact image of him. If the whole thing had been carefully studied, it could not have answered its purpose better. The owl stands quite perpendicular, presenting a front of light mottled gray; the eyes are closed to a mere slit, the ear-feathers depressed, the beak buried in the plumage, and the whole attitude is one of silent, motionless waiting and observation. If a mouse should be seen crossing the highway, or scudding over any exposed part of the snowy surface in the twilight, the owl would doubtless swoop down upon it. I think the owl has learned to distinguish me from the rest of the passers-by; at least, when I stop before him, and he sees himself observed, he backs down into his den, as I have said, in a very amusing manner. Whether bluebirds, nuthatches, and chickadees — birds that pass the night in cavities of trees — ever run into the clutches of the dozing owl, I should be glad to know. My impression is, however, that they seek out smaller cavities. An old willow by the roadside blew down one summer, and a decayed branch broke open, revealing a brood of half-fledged owls, and many feathers and quills of bluebirds, orioles, and other songsters, showing plainly enough why all birds fear and berate the owl.

The English house sparrows, which are so rapidly increasing among us, and which must add greatly to the food supply of the owls and other birds of prey, seek to baffle their enemies by roosting in the densest evergreens they can find, in the arbor-vitæ, and in hemlock hedges. Soft-winged as the owl is, he cannot steal in upon such a retreat without giving them warning.

These sparrows are becoming about the most noticeable of my winter neighbors, and a troop of them every morning watch me put out the hens' feed, and soon claim their share. I rather encouraged them in their neighborliness, till one day I discovered the snow under a favorite plum-tree where they most frequently perched covered with the scales of the fruit-buds. On investigating, I found that the tree had been nearly stripped of its buds, — a very unneighborly act on the part of the sparrows, considering, too, all the cracked corn I had scattered for them. So I at once served notice on them that our good understanding was at an end. And a hint is as good as a kick with this bird. The stone I hurled among them, and the one with which I followed them up, may have been taken as a kick; but they were only a hint of the shotgun that stood ready in the corner. The sparrows left in high dudgeon, and were not back again in some days, and were then very shy. No doubt the time is near at hand when we shall have to wage serious war upon these sparrows, as they long have had to do on the continent of Europe. And yet it will be hard to kill the little wretches, the only Old World birds we have. When I take down my gun to shoot them I shall probably remember that the Psalmist said, " I watch, and am as a sparrow alone upon the housetop," and maybe the recollection will cause me to stay my hand. The sparrows have the Old World hardiness and prolificness; they are wise and tenacious of life, and we shall find it by and by no small matter to keep them in check. Our native birds are much different, less prolific, less shrewd, less aggressive and persistent, less quick-witted and able to read the note of danger or hostility, — in short, less sophisticated. Most of our birds are yet essentially wild, that is, little changed by civilization. In winter, especially, they sweep by me and around me in flocks, — the Canada sparrow, the snow bunting, the shore lark, the pine grosbeak, the redpoll, the cedar-bird, — feeding upon frozen apples in the orchard, upon cedar-berries, upon maple-buds, and the berries of the mountain-ash, and the celtis, and upon the seeds of the weeds that rise above the snow in the fields, or upon the hay-seed dropped where the cattle have been foddered in the barnyard or about the distant stack ; but yet taking no heed of man, in no way changing their habits so as to take advantage of his presence in nature. The pine grosbeaks will come in numbers upon your porch to get the black drupes of the honeysuckle or the woodbine, or within reach of your windows to get the berries of the mountain-ash, but they know you not ; they look at you as innocently and unconcernedly as at a bear or moose in their native north, and your house is no more to them than a ledge of rocks.

The only ones of my winter neighbors that actually rap at my door are the nuthatches and wood-peckers, and these do not know that it is my door. My retreat is covered with the bark of young chest-nut-trees, and the birds, I suspect, mistake it for a huge stump that ought to hold fat grubs (there is not even a book-worm inside of it), and their loud rapping often makes me think I have a caller indeed. I place fragments of hickory-nuts in the interstices of the bark, and thus attract the nut-hatches ; a bone upon my window-sill attracts both nuthatches and the downy woodpecker. They peep in curiously through the window upon me, pecking away at my bone, too often a very poor one. A bone nailed to a tree a few feet in front of the window attracts crows as well as lesser birds. Even the slate-colored snowbird, a seed-eater, comes and nibbles it occasionally.

The bird that seems to consider he has the best right to the bone both upon the tree and upon the sill is the downy woodpecker, my favorite neighbor among the winter birds, to whom I will mainly devote the remainder of this chapter. His retreat is but a few paces from my own, in the decayed limb of an apple-tree, which he excavated several autumns ago. I say "he" because the red plume on the top of his head proclaims the sex. It seems not to be generally known to our writers upon ornithology that certain of our woodpeckers — probably all the winter residents — each fall excavate a limb or the trunk of a tree in which to pass the winter, and that the cavity is abandoned in the spring, probably for a new one in which nidification takes place. So far as I have observed, these cavities are drilled out only by the males. Where the females take up their quarters I am not so well informed, though I suspect that they use the abandoned holes of the males of the previous year.

The particular woodpecker to which I refer drilled his first hole in my apple-tree one fall four or five

years ago. This he occupied till the following spring,
when he abandoned it. The next fall he began a
hole in an adjoining limb, later than before, and
when it was about half completed a female took
possession of his old quarters. I am sorry to say
that this seemed to enrage the male very much, and
he persecuted the poor bird whenever she appeared
upon the scene. He would fly at her spitefully
and drive her off. One chilly November morning,
as I passed under the tree, I heard the hammer of
the little architect in his cavity, and at the same
time saw the persecuted female sitting at the entrance of the other hole as if she would fain come
out. She was actually shivering, probably from
both fear and cold. I understood the situation at
a glance; the bird was afraid to come forth and
brave the anger of the male. Not till I had rapped
smartly upon the limb with my stick did she come
out and attempt to escape; but she had not gone
ten feet from the tree before the male was in hot
pursuit, and in a few moments had driven her back
to the same tree, where she tried to avoid him
among the branches. A few days after, he rid himself of his unwelcome neighbor in the following
ingenious manner: he fairly scuttled the other cavity; he drilled a hole into the bottom of it that let
in the light and the cold, and I saw the female
there no more. I did not see him in the act of
rendering this tenement uninhabitable; but one

morning, behold it was punctured at the bottom, and the circumstances all seemed to point to him as the author of it. There is probably no gallantry among the birds except at the mating season. I have frequently seen the male woodpecker drive the female away from the bone upon the tree. When she hopped around to the other end and timidly nibbled it, he would presently dart spitefully at her. She would then take up her position in his rear and wait till he had finished his meal. The position of the female among the birds is very much the same as that of women among savage tribes. Most of the drudgery of life falls upon her, and the leavings of the males are often her lot.

My bird is a genuine little savage, doubtless, but I value him as a neighbor. It is a satisfaction during the cold or stormy winter nights to know he is warm and cozy there in his retreat. When the day is bad and unfit to be abroad in, he is there too. When I wish to know if he is at home, I go and rap upon his tree, and, if he is not too lazy or indifferent, after some delay he shows his head in his round doorway about ten feet above, and looks down inquiringly upon me, — sometimes latterly I think half resentfully, as much as to say, "I would thank you not to disturb me so often." After sundown, he will not put his head out any more when I call, but as I step away I can get a glimpse of him inside looking cold and reserved. He is a late riser, especially if it is a cold or disagreeable morning, in this respect being like the barn fowls; it is sometimes near nine o'clock before I see him leave his tree. On the other hand, he comes home early, being in, if the day is unpleasant, by four P. M. He lives all alone; in this respect I do not commend his example. Where his mate is, I should like to know.

I have discovered several other woodpeckers in adjoining orchards, each of which has a like home, and leads a like solitary life. One of them has excavated a dry limb within easy reach of my hand, doing the work also in September. But the choice of tree was not a good one; the limb was too much decayed, and the workman had made the cavity too large; a chip had come out, making a hole in the outer wall. Then he went a few inches down the limb and began again, and excavated a large, commodious chamber, but had again come too near the surface; scarcely more than the bark protected him in one place, and the limb was very much weakened. Then he made another attempt still farther down the limb, and drilled in an inch or two, but seemed to change his mind; the work stopped, and I concluded the bird had wisely abandoned the tree. Passing there one cold, rainy November day, I thrust in my two fingers and was surprised to feel something soft and warm: as I drew away my hand the bird came out, apparently no more surprised than I was. It had decided, then, to make its home in the old limb; a decision it had occasion to regret, for not long after, on a stormy night, the branch gave way and fell to the ground: —

"When the bough breaks the cradle will fall,
And down will come baby, cradle and all."

Such a cavity makes a snug, warm home, and when the entrance is on the under side of the limb, as is usual, the wind and snow cannot reach the occupant. Late in December, while crossing a high, wooded mountain, lured by the music of fox-hounds, I discovered fresh yellow chips strewing the new-fallen snow, and at once thought of my woodpeckers. On looking around I saw where one had been at work excavating a lodge in a small yellow birch. The orifice was about fifteen feet from the ground, and appeared as round as if struck with a compass. It was on the east side of the tree, so as to avoid the prevailing west and northwest winds. As it was nearly two inches in diameter, it could not have been the work of the downy, but must have been that of the hairy, or else the yellow-bellied woodpecker. His home had probably been wrecked by some violent wind, and he was thus providing himself another. In digging out these retreats the woodpeckers prefer a dry, brittle trunk, not too soft. They go in horizontally to the centre and then turn downward, enlarging the tunnel as they go, till when finished it is the shape of a long, deep pear.

Another trait our woodpeckers have that endears them to me, and that has never been pointedly noticed by our ornithologists, is their habit of drumming in the spring. They are songless birds, and yet all are musicians; they make the dry limbs eloquent of the coming change. Did you think that loud, sonorous hammering which proceeded from the orchard or from the near woods on that still March or April morning was only some bird getting its breakfast? It is downy, but he is not rapping at the door of a grub; he is rapping at the door of spring, and the dry limb thrills beneath the ardor of his blows. Or, later in the season, in the dense forest or by some remote mountain lake, does that measured rhythmic beat that breaks upon the silence, first three strokes following each other rapidly, succeeded by two louder ones with longer intervals between them, and that has an effect upon the alert ear as if the solitude itself had at last found a voice, — does that suggest anything less than a deliberate musical performance? In fact, our woodpeckers are just as characteristically drummers as is the ruffed grouse, and they have their particular limbs and stubs to which they resort for that purpose. Their need of expression is apparently just as great as that of the song-birds, and it is not surprising that they should have found out that there is music in a dry, seasoned limb which can be evoked beneath their beaks.

A few seasons ago, a downy woodpecker, probably the individual one who is now my winter neighbor, began to drum early in March in a partly decayed apple-tree that stands in the edge of a narrow strip of woodland near me. When the morning was still and mild I would often hear him through my window before I was up, or by half-past six o'clock, and he would keep it up pretty briskly till nine or ten o'clock, in this respect resembling the grouse, which do most of their drumming in the forenoon. His drum was the stub of a dry limb about the size of one's wrist. The heart was decayed and gone, but the outer shell was hard and resonant. The bird would keep his position there for an hour at a time. Between his drummings he would preen his plumage and listen as if for the response of the female, or for the drum of some rival. How swift his head would go when he was delivering his blows upon the limb! His beak wore the surface perceptibly. When he wished to change the key, which was quite often, he would shift his position an inch or two to a knot which gave out a higher, shriller note. When I climbed up to examine his drum, he was much disturbed. I did not know he was in the vicinity, but it seems he saw me from a near tree, and came in haste to the neighboring branches, and with spread plumage and a sharp note demanded plainly enough what my business was with his drum. I was invading his privacy, desecrating his shrine, and the bird was much put out. After some weeks the female appeared; he had literally drummed up a mate; his urgent and oft-repeated advertisement was answered. Still the drumming did not cease, but was quite as fervent as before. If a mate could be won by drumming, she could be kept and entertained by more drumming; courtship should not end with marriage. If the bird felt musical before, of course he felt much more so now. Besides that, the gentle deities needed propitiating in behalf of the nest and young as well as in behalf of the mate. After a time a second female came, when there was war between the two. I did not see them come to blows, but I saw one female pursuing the other about the place, and giving her no rest for several days. She was evidently trying to run her out of the neighborhood. Now and then, she, too, would drum briefly, as if sending a triumphant message to her mate.

The woodpeckers do not each have a particular dry limb to which they resort at all times to drum, like the one I have described. The woods are full of suitable branches, and they drum more or less here and there as they are in quest of food; yet I am convinced each one has its favorite spot, like the grouse, to which it resorts especially in the morning. The sugar-maker in the maple-woods may notice that this sound proceeds from the same tree or trees about his camp with great regularity. A woodpecker in my vicinity has drummed for two seasons on a telegraph pole, and he makes the wires and glass insulators ring. Another drums on a thin board on the end of a long grape-arbor, and on still mornings can be heard a long distance.

A friend of mine in a Southern city tells me of a red-headed woodpecker that drums upon a lightning-rod on his neighbor's house. Nearly every clear, still morning at certain seasons, he says, this musical rapping may be heard. "He alternates his tapping with his stridulous call, and the effect on a cool, autumn-like morning is very pleasing."

The high-hole appears to drum more promiscuously than does downy. He utters his long, loud spring call, *whick — whick — whick — whick*, and then begins to rap with his beak upon his perch before the last note has reached your ear. I have seen him drum sitting upon the ridge of the barn. The log-cock, or pileated woodpecker, the largest and wildest of our Northern species, I never have heard drum. His blows should wake the echoes.

When the woodpecker is searching for food, or laying siege to some hidden grub, the sound of his hammer is dead or muffled, and is heard but a few yards. It is only upon dry, seasoned timber, freed of its bark, that he beats his reveille to spring and wooes his mate.

Wilson was evidently familiar with this vernal drumming of the woodpeckers, but quite misinterprets it. Speaking of the red-bellied species, he says : " It rattles like the rest of the tribe on the dead limbs, and with such violence as to be heard in still weather more than half a mile off ; and listens to hear the insect it has alarmed." He listens rather to hear the drum of his rival, or the brief and coy response of the female; for there are no insects in these dry limbs.

On one occasion I saw downy at his drum when a female flew quickly through the tree and alighted a few yards beyond him. He paused instantly, and kept his place apparently without moving a muscle. The female, I took it, had answered his advertisement. She flitted about from limb to limb (the female may be known by the absence of the crimson spot on the back of the head), apparently full of business of her own, and now and then would drum in a shy, tentative manner. The male watched her a few moments, and, convinced perhaps that she meant business, struck up his liveliest tune, then listened for her response. As it came back timidly but promptly, he left his perch and sought a nearer acquaintance with the prudent female. Whether or not a match grew out of this little flirtation I cannot say.

The downy woodpeckers are sometimes accused of injuring the apple and other fruit trees, but the depredator is probably the larger and rarer yellow-bellied species. One autumn I caught one of these fellows in the act of sinking long rows of his little wells in the limb of an apple-tree. There were series of rings of them, one above another, quite around the stem, some of them the third of an inch across. They are evidently made to get at the tender, juicy bark, or cambium layer, next to the hard wood of the tree. The health and vitality of the branch are so seriously impaired by them that it often dies.

In the following winter the same bird (probably) tapped a maple-tree in front of my window in fifty-six places; and when the day was sunny, and the sap oozed out, he spent most of his time there. He knew the good sap-days, and was on hand promptly for his tipple; cold and cloudy days he did not appear. He knew which side of the tree to tap, too, and avoided the sunless northern expos-ure. When one series of well-holes failed to sup-ply him, he would sink another, drilling through the bark with great ease and quickness. Then, when the day was warm, and the sap ran freely, he would have a regular sugar-maple debauch, sitting there by his wells hour after hour, and as fast as they became filled sipping out the sap. This he did in a gentle, caressing manner that was very suggestive. He made a row of wells near the foot of the tree, and other rows higher up, and he would hop up and down the trunk as these became filled. He would hop down the tree backward with the utmost ease, throwing his tail outward and his head inward at each hop. When the wells would freeze up or his thirst become slaked, he would ruffle his feathers, draw himself together, and sit and doze in the sun on the side of the tree. He passed the night in a hole in an apple-tree not far off. He was evidently a young bird, not yet having the plumage of the mature male or female, and yet he knew which tree to tap and where to tap it. I saw where he had bored several maples in the vicinity, but no oaks or chestnuts. I nailed up a fat bone near his sap-works: the downy woodpecker came there several times a day to dine; the nuthatch came, and even the snowbird took a taste occasionally; but this sapsucker never touched it; the sweet of the tree sufficed for him. This woodpecker does not breed or abound in my vicinity; only stray specimens are now and then to be met with in the colder months. As spring approached, the one I refer to took his departure.

I must bring my account of my neighbor in the tree down to the latest date; so after the lapse of a year I add the following notes. The last day of February was bright and spring-like. I heard the first sparrow sing that morning and the first scream-

ing of the circling hawks, and about seven o'clock
the first drumming of my little friend. His first
notes were uncertain and at long intervals, but by
and by he warmed up and beat a lively tattoo. As
the season advanced he ceased to lodge in his old
quarters. I would rap and find nobody at home.
Was he out on a lark, I said, the spring fever
working in his blood? After a time his drumming
grew less frequent, and finally, in the middle of
April, ceased entirely. Had some accident befallen
him, or had he wandered away to fresh fields, following some siren of his species? Probably the
latter. Another bird that I had under observation
also left his winter-quarters in the spring. This,
then, appears to be the usual custom. The wrens
and the nuthatches and chickadees succeed to these
abandoned cavities, and often have amusing dis-
putes over them. The nuthatches frequently pass
the night in them, and the wrens and chickadees
nest in them. I have further observed that in excavating a cavity for a nest the downy woodpecker
makes the entrance smaller than when he is excavating his winter-quarters. This is doubtless for
the greater safety of the young birds.

The next fall the downy excavated another limb
in the old apple-tree, but had not got his retreat
quite finished when the large hairy woodpecker
appeared upon the scene. I heard his loud *click*,
click, early one frosty November morning. There

was something impatient and angry in the tone that arrested my attention. I saw the bird fly to the tree where downy had been at work, and fall with great violence upon the entrance to his cavity. The bark and the chips flew beneath his vigorous blows, and, before I fairly woke up to what he was doing, he had completely demolished the neat, round doorway of downy. He had made a large, ragged opening, large enough for himself to enter. I drove him away and my favorite came back, but only to survey the ruins of his castle for a moment and then go away. He lingered about for a day or two and then disappeared. The big hairy usurper passed a night in the cavity; but on being hustled out of it the next night by me, he also left, but not till he had demolished the entrance to a cavity in a neighboring tree where downy and his mate had reared their brood that summer, and where I had hoped the female would pass the winter.

VIII

A SALT BREEZE

WHEN one first catches the smell of the sea, his lungs seem involuntarily to expand, the same as they do when he steps into the open air after long confinement indoors. On the beach he is simply emerging into a larger and more primitive out of doors. There before him is aboriginal space, and the breath of it thrills and dilates his body. He stands at the open door of the continent and eagerly drinks the large air. This breeze savors of the original element; it is a breath out of the morning of the world, — bitter, but so fresh and tonic! He has taken salt grossly and at second hand all his days; now let him inhale it at the fountain-head, and let its impalpable crystals penetrate his spirit, and prick and chafe him into new activity.

We Americans are great eaters of salt, probably the largest eaters of salt and drinkers of water of any of the civilized peoples ; the amount of the former consumed annually *per capita* being more than double the amount consumed in England and on the Continent; and the quantity of water (with ice in it) we drink is in still greater proportions.

159

Our dry climate calls for the water, and probably
our nervous, dyspeptic tendencies for the salt.
Hence our need, as a people, of that great tonic
and sedative, the seashore. In Biblical times, new-
born babies were rubbed with salt. I suppose it
stimulated them and quickened their circulation.
American babies are not thus rubbed, and there
comes a time with most of us when we feel that
the operation cannot be put off any longer, and we
rush down to the sea to have the service performed
by the old nurse herself, and the pores of both
mind and body well cleansed and opened.

Nothing about the sea is more impressive than
its ceaseless rocking. Without either wind or tide,
it would probably be restless and oscillating, because it registers and passes along the fluctuations
of the earthy crust. The solid ground is only relatively solid. The scientists, under the direction of
the British Association, who sought to determine
the influence of the moon upon the earth's crust,
found, as soon as their instruments were delicate
enough to register the influence of that body, many
other agencies at work. They could find no really
solid spot to plant their instruments upon. Thus,
over the area of a high barometer, the earth's crust
bent beneath the weight of the column of air. At
sea the waters are pressed down. The waves of
the atmospheric ocean, as they sweep around the
earth in vast alternations, cause both land and

water to rise and fall as beneath the tread of some striding Colossus. This unequal barometric pressure over the Atlantic area would, doubtless, of itself keep its equilibrium perpetually disturbed. Thus, "the cradle endlessly rocking," of which our poet sings, is not only bestrode by the winds and swung by the punctual hand of the tides, but the fairest summer weather gives it a nudge, and the bending floor beneath it contributes an impulse. Its rocking is secured beyond peradventure. Darwin seems to think it is the cradle where the primordial life of the globe had its infancy, — a conclusion of science anticipated by an old Greek poet who said, —

"Ocean, father of gods and men."

Whether or not it rocked man, or the germ of man, into being, there can be little doubt that it will continue to rock after he and all things else are wrapped in the final sleep.

Its grandest swing, I found during a couple of weeks' sojourn upon the coast, is often upon a fair day. Local winds and storms make it spiteful and angry. They break up and scatter the waves; but some quiet morning you saunter down to the beach and find the sea beating its long roll. The waves run parallel to the shore and come in with great regularity and deliberation, falling upon it in a succession of long, low cataracts, and you realize the

161

force of the Homeric epithet, "the far-resounding sea." It is a sort of prostrate Niagara expiring in intermittent torrents. Often there is a marked explosion from the compression of the air in the hollow cylinder of the curling wave. These long swells are of the character of those which in the Hudson follow the passage of one of the great steamers, — large, measured, uniform. Something here has passed, probably a cyclone far at sea; and these breakers, with their epic swing, are the echo of its retreating footsteps.

Nothing is more singular and unexpected to the landsman than the combing of the waves, — a momentary perpendicular or incurving wall of water, a few yards from shore, with other water spilling or pouring over it as over a milldam, thus exhibiting for an instant a clear, perfectly formed cataract. But instantly the wall crumbles, or is crushed down, and in place of it there is a wild caldron of foaming, boiling water and sand.

There seems to be something more cosmic, or shall I say astronomic, in the sea than in the shore. Here you behold the round back of the globe: the lines are planetary. You feel that here is the true surface of the sphere, the curving, delicate sides of this huge bubble. On the land, amid the wrinkles of the hills, you have place, fixedness, locality, a nook in the chimney-corner; but upon the sea you are literally adrift; place is not, boundaries are not, space is vacant. You are upon the smooth disk of the planet, like a man bestriding the moon. Under your feet runs the line of the earth's rotundity, and round about you the same curve bounds your vision.

Then the sea brings us nearer that time when the earth was without form and void, — a vast, shoreless, and therefore voiceless, sea. You look upon the youth of the world; there is no age, no change, no decay here. It is older than the continents, and, in a measure, their creator. That it should devour them again, like Saturn his children, only adds to our sense of its mystery and power.

The sea is another firmament. The land is fugitive: it abides not. Vast areas have been scalped by the winds and the rains; but the sea, whose law is mutation, changes not, — type of fickleness and instability ; yet the granite crumbles, and it remains the same. The semicircle that bounds your view seaward, and that travels with you along the beach, a vast, liquid crescent or half-moon, upon the inner, jagged edge of which you stand, is the type of that which changes not, which neither ends nor begins, and into which all form and all being merge.

This is a part of the vague fascination of the shore ; 't is the boundary of two worlds. With your feet upon the present, you confront aboriginal time and space. If we could reach the point in the horizon where the earth and sky meet, we might find the same fascination there. In the absence of this the best substitute is the beach.

We seem to breathe a larger air on the coast. It is the place for large types, large thoughts. 'T is not farms, or a township, we see now, but God's own domain. Possession, ownership, civilization, boundary lines cease, and there within reach is a clear page of terrestrial space, as unmarred and as unmarrable as if plucked from the sidereal heavens.

How inviting and adventurous the ships look, dropping behind the rim of the horizon, or gently blown along its edge, their yard-arms pointing to all quarters of the globe! Mystery, adventure, the promise of unknown lands, beckon to us from the full-rigged ships. One does not see them come or depart; they dawn upon him like his own thoughts, some dim and shadowy, just hovering on the verge of consciousness, others white and full, a solace to the eye. But presently, while you ponder, they are gone, or else vaguely notch the horizon-line. Illusion, enchantment, hover over the sail-ships. They have the charm of the ancient world of fable and romance. They are blown by Homeric winds. They are a survival from the remotest times. But yonder comes a black steamship, cutting across this enchanted circle in defiance of wind and tide; this is the modern world snubbing and dispelling our illusions, and putting our poets to flight.

But the veritable oceanic brine there before one, the continental, primordial, original liquid, the hoary, eternal sea itself, — what can a lover of fields and woods make of it? None of the charms or solacements of birds and flowers here, or of rural sights and sounds; no repose, no plaintiveness, no dumb companionship; but a spirit threatening, hungering, remorseless, decoying, fascinating, serpentine, rebelling and forever rebelling against the fiat, "Thus far shalt thou come, and no farther." The voice of the sea is unlike any other sound in nature; more riant and chafing than any roar of woods or storms. One never ceases to hear the briny, rimy, weltering quality, — it is salt to the ear no less than to the smell. One fancies he hears the friction and clashing of the invisible crystals. A shooting avalanche of snow might have this frosty, beaded, anfractuous sound. The sands and pebbles and broken shells have something to do with it; but without these that threatening, serrated edge remains, — the grainy, saline voice of the sea.

'T is a pity the fabulous sea-serpent is not a reality. The sea seems to imply such a monster, swimming as a leech swims, with vertical undulations, splitting the waves, or reposing across them in vast scaly coils. There is something in the sea that fills the imagination of men with the image of these things. The sea-serpent will always be seen by somebody, because the sea itself is serpentine, — a writhing, crawling, crested, glistening saurian with the globe in its embrace. How it rises up and darts upon you! In storms, its breath blackens and blights the shore vegetation; it devours the beach and disgorges it again, and piles the shore with foam, like masses of unwashed wool. Often a hissing, sibilant sound seems to issue from under the edge of the bursting wave. Then that ever-recurring rustle calls up a vision of some scaly monster uncoiling or measuring its length upon the sands. I was told of two girls, in bathing-suits, sitting upon the beach, where the waves, which were running very high, reached them with only their laced and embroidered edges; then, as if it had been getting ready for a spring, a huge wave rushed up and snatched them both into the sea, and they were drowned. In a few days the body of one was cast up, but the other was never seen again. Such fawning, such treachery, are in the waves.

The sea shifts its pillow like an uneasy sleeper. The contour of the beach is seldom two days alike; that round, smooth bolster of sand is at times very prominent. The waves stroke and caress it, and slide their delicate sea-draperies over it, as if they were indeed making their bed. When you walk

166

there again it is gone, carried down under the waves, and the beach is low and naked.

Both the sight and the sound of the waves fill the mind with images. One thinks of rockets, windrows, embroideries. How they lift themselves up and grow tall as they approach the shore! They are entering shallower water, they are running aground, and they rise up like vessels.

I saw little in the waves that suggested steeds, but more that reminded of huge sheep. At times they would come wallowing ashore precisely like a great flock or mob of woolly-headed sheep. The wave breaks far out, and then comes that rushing line of tossing, leaping woolly heads and shoulders, diminishing as it comes, and leaving the space behind it strewn with foam. Sometimes the waves look like revolving cylindrical knives, carving the coast. Then they thrust up their thin, crescent-shaped edges, like reapers, reaping only shells and sand ; yet one seems to hear the hiss of a great sickle, the crackle of stubble, the rustle of sheaves, and the screening of grain. Then again there is mimic thunder as the waves burst, followed by a sound like the downpouring of torrents of rain. How it shovels the sand and sifts and washes it forever! Every particle of silt goes seaward ; it is the earth-pollen with which the sunken floors of the sea are deeply covered. What material for future continents, new worlds and new peoples, is hoarded within its sunless depths! How Darwin longed to read the sealed book of the earth's history that lies buried beneath the sea! He thought it probable that the first continents were there ; that the areas of elevation and of subsidence had changed places in the remote past.

Turning over the collections of sea-poetry in the libraries, it is rare enough to find a line or a stanza with the real savor of the shore in it. 'T is mostly fresh-water poetry, very pretty, often spirited and frothy, but seldom gritty, saline, and elemental. That bearded, bristling, savage quality of the sea, to which I have referred, you shall hardly find hinted at, except, perhaps, in Whitman, who is usually ignored in these anthologies. Tennyson's touches, as here and there in " Sea-Dreams," always satisfy, and one chafes that Shakespeare should have left so little on the subject.

The poets make a dead set at the vastness, power, and terror of the sea, and take their fill of these aspects of it. 'T is an easy theme, and soon wearies. We crave the verse that shall give us the taste of the salt spray upon our lips. Bryant's hymn to the sea is noble and stately, but it is only his forest hymn shifted to the shore. It touches the same chords. It has no marine quality or atmosphere. The bitterness and the sweetness of the sea, as of a celestial dragon devouring and purifying, are not in it. The poet wings his lofty flight above

sea and shore alike. When Emerson sings of the
sea, there is more savor, more tonic air, a closer
and stronger hold upon the subject; but even he
takes refuge in the vastness of his theme, and speaks
through the imperial voice of the sea : —

> " I heard, or seemed to hear, the chiding Sea
> Say, Pilgrim, why so late and slow to come?
> Am I not always here, thy summer home?
> Is not my voice thy music, morn and eve,
> My breath thy healthful climate in the heats,
> My touch thy antidote, my bay thy bath?
> Was ever building like my terraces?
> Was ever couch magnificent as mine? "

There are strong lines in Rossetti's "Sea Lim-
its," but, like the others, it is a far-off idealization
of the subject, and does not bring one nearer the
sea.

There are occasionally good descriptive lines in
Miller, as

> " I crossed the hilly sea."

And again, —

> " The ships, black-bellied, climb the sea."

There is something fresh and inviting in this
comparison : —

> " As pure as sea-washed sands."

But when the poet of the Sierras places old Nep-
tune on the anxious bench, in this wise, —

"Behold the ocean on the beach
    Kneel lowly down as if in prayer;
    I hear a moan as of despair,
    While far at sea do toss and reach
    Some things so like white pleading hands,"

one has serious qualms.

The breakers usually suggest to the poets rearing and plunging steeds, as in Arnold : —

"Now the wild white horses play,
    Champ and chafe and toss in the spray;"

and Stedman's spirited poem, "Surf," makes use of the same image. Byron, in "Childe Harold," lays his hand upon the "mane" of the ocean. Whitman, recalling the shapes and sounds of the shore by moonlight, startles the imagination with this line : —

"The white arms out in the breakers tirelessly tossing."

One of our poets — Taylor, I think — has applied the epithet "chameleon" to the sea, — "the chameleon sea," — which fits well, for the sea takes on all hues and tints. To the genial Autocrat the sea is "feline" and treacherous, — something of the crouching and leaping tiger in it. The poet of "The New Day," as a foil to his love and admiration for it, calls it "the accursed sea." There is sea-salt in Whitman's poetry, strongly realistic epithets and phrases, that had their birth upon the shore,

and that perpetually recur to one as he saunters on
the beach. He uses the word "rustling" and the
phrase "hoarse and sibilant" to describe the sound
of the waves. "The husky-voiced sea" expresses
the saline quality to which I have referred : —

"Sea of stretch'd ground-swells,
Sea breathing broad and convulsive breaths,
Sea of the brine of life, and of unshovell'd yet always
     ready graves,
Howler and scooper of storms, capricious and dainty sea,
I am integral with you; I too am of one phase and of all
     phases."

     "Oh, madly the sea pushes upon the land,
       With love, with love."

Or this, written upon the beach at Ocean Grove
in 1883, —

"With husky-haughty lips, O Sea!
Where day and night I wend thy surf-beat shore,
Imaging to my sense thy varied strange suggestions,
The troops of white-maned racers racing to the goal,
Thy ample smiling face, dash'd with the sparkling
     dimples of the sun,
Thy brooding scowl and murk — thy unloos'd hurricanes,
Thy unsubduedness, caprices, wilfulness;
Great as thou art above the rest, thy many tears — a lack
     from all eternity in thy content
(Naught but the greatest struggles, wrongs, defeats, could
     make thee greatest — no less could make thee),

Thy lonely state — something thou ever seek'st and
    seek'st, yet never gain'st,
Surely some right withheld — some voice, in huge monot-
    onous rage, of freedom-lover pent,
Some vast heart, like a planet's, chain'd and chafing in
    those breakers,
By lengthen'd swell, and spasm, and panting breath,
And rhythmic rasping of thy sands and waves,
And serpent hiss, and savage peals of laughter,
And undertones of distant lion roar
(Sounding, appealing to the sky's deaf ear — but now,
    rapport for once,
A phantom in the night thy confidant for once),
The first and last confession of the globe,
Outsurging, muttering from thy soul's abysms,
The tale of cosmic elemental passion,
Thou tellest to a kindred soul."

Whitman is essentially of the shore; his bearded,
aboriginal quality, — something in his words that
smites and chafes, a tonic like salt air, not sweet, but
dilating; his irregular, flowing, repeating, elliptical
lines; his sense of space, and constant reference to
the earth and the orbs as standards and symbols.
His poems are rarely architectural or sculpturesque,
either to the eye or to the mind; no carving and
shaping merely for art's sake; but floating, drifting,
surging masses of concrete events and images, more
or less nebular, protoplasmic, and preliminary, but
always potent and alive, and full of the salt of the

earth, holding in solution as no other poet does his times and country.

The sea is the great purifier and equalizer of climes, the great canceler, leveler, distributer, neutralizer, and sponge of oblivion. What a cemetery, and yet what healing in its breath! What a desert, and yet what plenty in its depths! How destructive, and yet the continents are its handiwork!

> "Sea, full of food, the nourisher of kinds,
> Purger of earth, and medicine of men."

And yet famine and thirst, dismay and death, stalk the wave. Contradictory, multitudinous sea! the despoiler and yet the renewer; barren as a rock, yet as fruitful as a field; old as Time, and young as to-day; merciless as Fate, and tender as Love; the fountain of all waters, yet mocking its victims with the most horrible thirst; smiting like a hammer, and caressing like a lady's palm; falling upon the shore like a wall of rock, then creeping up the sands as with the rustle of an infant's drapery; cesspool of the continents, yet " creating a sweet clime by its breath; " pit of terrors, gulf of despair, caldron of hell, yet health, power, beauty, enchantment, dwell forever with the sea.

IX

A SPRING RELISH

IT is a little remarkable how regularly severe and mild winters alternate in our climate for a series of years, — a feminine and a masculine one, as it were, almost invariably following each other. Every other season now for ten years the ice-gatherers on the river have been disappointed of a full harvest, and every other season the ice has formed from fifteen to twenty inches thick. From 1873 to 1884 there was no marked exception to this rule. But in the last-named year, when, according to the succession, a mild winter was due, the breed seemed to have got crossed, and a sort of mongrel winter was the result; neither mild nor severe, but very stormy, capricious, and disagreeable, with ice a foot thick on the river. The winter which followed, that of 1884–85, though slow and hesitating at first, fully proved itself as belonging to the masculine order. The present winter of 1885–86 shows a marked return to the type of two years ago, less hail and snow, but by no means the mild season that was due. By and by, probably, the meteorological influences will get back into the old ruts again,

175

and we shall have once more the regular alternation of mild and severe winters. During very open winters, like that of 1879–80, nature in my latitude, eighty miles north of New York, hardly shuts up house at all. That season I heard a little piping frog on the 7th of December, and on the 18th of January, in a spring run, I saw the common bullfrog out of his hibernaculum, evidently thinking it was spring. A copperhead snake was killed here about the same date; caterpillars did not seem to retire, as they usually do, but came forth every warm day. The note of the bluebird was heard nearly every week all winter, and occasionally that of the robin. Such open winters make one fear that his appetite for spring will be blunted when spring really does come ; but he usually finds that the April days have the old relish. April is that part of the season that never cloys upon the palate. It does not surfeit one with good things, but provokes and stimulates the curiosity. One is on the alert, there are hints and suggestions on every hand. Something has just passed, or stirred, or called, or breathed, in the open air or in the ground about, that we would fain know more of. May is sweet, but April is pungent. There is frost enough in it to make it sharp, and heat enough in it to make it quick.

In my walks in April, I am on the lookout for watercress. It is a plant that has the pungent

176

A SPRING RELISH

April flavor. In many parts of the country the watercress seems to have become completely naturalized, and is essentially a wild plant. I found it one day in a springy place, on the top of a high, wooded mountain, far from human habitation. We gathered it and ate it with our sandwiches. Where the walker cannot find this salad, a good substitute may be had in our native spring cress, which is also in perfection in April. Crossing a wooded hill in the regions of the Catskills on the 15th of the month, I found a purple variety of the plant, on the margin of a spring that issued from beneath a ledge of rocks, just ready to bloom. I gathered the little white tubers, that are clustered like miniature potatoes at the root, and ate them, and they were a surprise and a challenge to the tongue ; on the table they would well fill the place of mustard, and horseradish, and other appetizers. When I was a schoolboy, we used to gather, in a piece of woods on our way to school, the roots of the closely allied species to eat with our lunch. But we generally ate them up before lunch-time. Our name for this plant was "Crinkle-root." The botanists call it the toothwort (*Dentaria*), also pepper-root.

From what fact or event shall one really date the beginning of spring? The little piping frogs usually furnish a good starting-point. One spring I heard the first note on the 6th of April; the next on the 27th of February; but in reality the latter

177

season was only about two weeks earlier than the
former. When the bees carry in their first pollen,
one would think spring had come; yet this fact
does not always correspond with the real stage of
the season. Before there is any bloom anywhere,
bees will bring pollen to the hive. Where do they
get it?

I have seen them gathering it on the fresh sawdust in the woodyard, especially on that of hickory
or maple. They wallow amid the dust, working
it over and over, and searching it like diamond-
hunters, and after a time their baskets are filled
with the precious flour, which is probably only a
certain part of the wood, doubtless the soft, nutri-
tious inner bark.

In fact, all signs and phases of life in the early
season are very capricious, and are earlier or later
just as some local or exceptional circumstance
favors or hinders. It is only such birds as arrive
after about the 20th of April that are at all " punctual" according to the almanac. I never have
known the arrival of the barn swallow to vary
much from that date in this latitude, no matter
how early or late the season might be. Another
punctual bird is the yellow red-poll warbler, the
first of his class that appears. Year after year, between the 20th and the 25th, I am sure to see this
little bird about my place for a day or two only,
now on the ground, now on the fences, now on the

small trees and shrubs, and closely examining the
buds or just-opening leaves of the apple-trees. He
is a small olive-colored bird, with a dark-red or
maroon-colored patch on the top of his head. His
ordinary note is a smart " chirp." His movements
are very characteristic, especially that vertical, oscillating movement of the hind part of his body,
like that of the wagtails. There are many birds
that do not come here till May, be the season never
so early. The spring of 1878 was very forward,
and on the 27th of April I made this entry in my
note-book: " In nature it is the middle of May,
and, judging from vegetation alone, one would expect to find many of the later birds, as the oriole,
the wood thrush, the kingbird, the catbird, the
tanager, the indigo-bird, the vireos, and many of
the warblers, but they have not arrived. The May
birds, it seems, will not come in April, no matter
how the season favors."

Some birds passing north in the spring are pro-
vokingly silent. Every April I see the hermit
thrush hopping about the woods, and in case of a
sudden snow-storm seeking shelter about the outbuildings; but I never hear even a fragment of his
wild, silvery strain. The white-crowned sparrow
also passes in silence. I see the bird for a few
days about the same date each year, but he will
not reveal to me his song. On the other hand,
his congener, the white-throated sparrow, is decid-

edly musical in passing, both spring and fall. His sweet, wavering whistle is at times quite as full and perfect as when heard in June or July in the Canadian woods. The latter bird is much more numerous than the white-crowned, and its stay with us more protracted, which may in a measure account for the greater frequency of its song. The fox sparrow, who passes earlier (sometimes in March), is also chary of the music with which he is so richly endowed. It is not every season that I hear him, though my ear is on the alert for his strong, finely modulated whistle.

Nearly all the warblers sing in passing. I hear them in the orchards, in the groves, in the woods, as they pause to feed in their northward journey, their brief, lisping, shuffling, insect-like notes requiring to be searched for by the ear, as their forms by the eye. But the ear is not tasked to identify the songs of the kinglets, as they tarry briefly with us in spring. In fact, there is generally a week in April or early May, —

> " On such a time as goes before the leaf,
> When all the woods stand in a mist of green
> And nothing perfect,''

during which the piping, voluble, rapid, intricate, and delicious warble of the ruby-crowned kinglet is the most noticeable strain to be heard, especially among the evergreens.

A SPRING RELISH

I notice that during the mating season of the birds the rivalries and jealousies are not all confined to the males. Indeed, the most spiteful and furious battles, as among the domestic fowls, are frequently between females. I have seen two hen robins scratch and pull feathers in a manner that contrasted strongly with the courtly and dignified sparring usual between the males. One March a pair of bluebirds decided to set up housekeeping in the trunk of an old apple-tree near my house. Not long after, an unwedded female appeared, and probably tried to supplant the lawful wife. I did not see what arts she used, but I saw her being very roughly handled by the jealous bride. The battle continued nearly all day about the orchard and grounds, and was a battle at very close quarters. The two birds would clinch in the air or on a tree, and fall to the ground with beaks and claws locked. The male followed them about, and warbled and called, but whether deprecatingly or encouragingly, I could not tell. Occasionally, he would take a hand, but whether to separate them, or whether to fan the flames, that I could not tell. So far as I could see, he was highly amused, and culpably indifferent to the issue of the battle.

The English spring begins much earlier than ours in New England and New York, yet an exceptionally early April with us must be nearly, if not quite, abreast with April as it usually appears in

England. The black-thorn sometimes blooms in Britain in February, but the swallow does not appear till about the 20th of April, nor the anemone bloom ordinarily till that date. The nightingale comes about the same time, and the cuckoo follows close. Our cuckoo does not come till near June; but the water-thrush, which Audubon thought nearly equal to the nightingale as a songster (though it certainly is not), I have known to come by the 21st. I have seen the sweet English violet, escaped from the garden, and growing wild by the roadside, in bloom on the 25th of March, which is about its date of flowering at home. During the same season, the first of our native flowers to appear was the hepatica, which I found on April 4. The arbutus and the dicentra appeared on the 10th, and the coltsfoot — which, however, is an importation — about the same time. The bloodroot, claytonia, saxifrage, and anemone were in bloom on the 17th, and I found the first blue violet and the great spurred violet on the 19th (saw the little violet-colored butterfly dancing about the woods the same day). I plucked my first dandelion on a meadow slope on the 23d, and in the woods, protected by a high ledge, my first trillium. During the month at least twenty native shrubs and wild flowers bloomed in my vicinity, which is an unusual showing for April.

There are many things left for May, but nothing

fairer than, if as fair as, the first flower, the hepatica. I find I never have admired this little firstling half enough. When at the maturity of its charms, it is certainly the gem of the woods. What an individuality it has! No two clusters alike ; all shades and sizes ; some are snow-white, some pale pink, with just a tinge of violet, some deep purple, others the purest blue, others blue touched with lilac. A solitary blue-purple one, fully expanded and rising over the brown leaves or the green moss, its cluster of minute anthers showing like a group of pale stars on its little firmament, is enough to arrest and hold the dullest eye. Then, as I have elsewhere stated, there are individual hepaticas, or individual families among them, that are sweet-scented. The gift seems as capricious as the gift of genius in families. You cannot tell which the fragrant ones are till you try them. Sometimes it is the large white ones, sometimes the large purple ones, sometimes the small pink ones. The odor is faint, and recalls that of the sweet violets. A correspondent, who seems to have carefully observed these fragrant hepaticas, writes me that this gift of odor is constant in the same plant ; that the plant which bears sweet-scented flowers this year will bear them next.

There is a brief period in our spring when I like more than at any other time to drive along the country roads, or even to be shot along by steam and have the landscape presented to me like a

map. It is at that period, usually late in April, when
we behold the first quickening of the earth. The
waters have subsided, the roads have become dry,
the sunshine has grown strong and its warmth has
penetrated the sod; there is a stir of preparation
about the farm and all through the country. One
does not care to see things very closely; his interest
in nature is not special but general. The earth is
coming to life again. All the genial and more fertile places in the landscape are brought out; the
earth is quickened in spots and streaks ; you can
see at a glance where man and nature have dealt
the most kindly with it. The warm, moist places,
the places that have had the wash of some building or of the road, or have been subjected to some
special mellowing influence, how quickly the turf
awakens there and shows the tender green! See
what the landscape would be, how much earlier
spring would come to it, if every square yard of it
were alike moist and fertile. As the later snows lay
in patches here and there, so now the earliest ver-
dure is irregularly spread over the landscape, and
is especially marked on certain slopes, as if it had
blown over from the other side and lodged there.

A little earlier the homesteads looked cold and
naked; the old farmhouse was bleak and unattrac-
tive; now Nature seems especially to smile upon it;
her genial influences crowd up around it; the turf
awakens all about as if in the spirit of friendliness.

184

A SPRING RELISH

See the old barn on the meadow-slope; the green seems to have oozed out from it, and to have flowed slowly down the hill; at a little distance it is lost in the sere stubble. One can see where every spring lies buried about the fields; its influence is felt at the surface, and the turf is early quickened there. Where the cattle have loved to lie and ruminate in the warm summer twilight, there the April sunshine loves to linger too, till the sod thrills to new life.

The home, the domestic feeling in nature, is brought out and enhanced at this time; what man has done tells, especially what he has done well. Our interest centres in the farmhouses, and in the influence that seems to radiate from there. The older the home, the more genial nature looks about it. The new architectural place of the rich citizen, with the barns and outbuildings concealed or disguised as much as possible, — spring is in no hurry about it; the sweat of long years of honest labor has not yet fattened the soil it stands upon.

The full charm of this April landscape is not brought out till the afternoon. It seems to need the slanting rays of the evening sun to give it the right mellowness and tenderness, or the right perspective. It is, perhaps, a little too bald in the strong, white light of the earlier part of the day; but when the faint, four-o'clock shadows begin to come out, and we look through the green vistas, and along the farm lanes toward the west, or out across long stretches of fields above which spring seems fairly hovering, just ready to alight, and note the teams slowly plowing, the brightened mould-board gleaming in the sun now and then, — it is at such times we feel its fresh, delicate attraction the most. There is no foliage on the trees yet; only here and there the red bloom of the soft maple, illuminated by the declining sun, shows vividly against the tender green of a slope beyond, or a willow, like a thin veil, stands out against a leafless wood. Here and there a little meadow water-course is golden with marsh marigolds, or some fence border, or rocky streak of neglected pasture land, is thickly starred with the white flowers of the bloodroot. The eye can devour a succession of landscapes at such a time; there is nothing that sates or entirely fills it, but every spring token stimulates it and makes it more on the alert.

April, too, is the time to go budding. A swelling bud is food for the fancy, and often food for the eye. Some buds begin to glow as they begin to swell. The bud scales change color and become a delicate rose pink. I note this especially in the European maple. The bud scales flush as if the effort to "keep in" brought the blood into their faces. The scales of the willow do not flush, but shine like ebony, and each one presses like a hand upon the catkin that will escape from beneath it.

When spring pushes pretty hard, many buds

begin to sweat as well as to glow; they exude a brown, fragrant, gummy substance that affords the honey-bee her first cement and hive varnish. The hickory, the horse-chestnut, the plane-tree, the poplars, are all coated with this April myrrh. That of certain poplars, like the Balm of Gilead, is the most noticeable and fragrant. No spring incense more agreeable. Its perfume is often upon the April breeze. I pick up the bud scales of the poplars along the road, long brown scales like the beaks of birds, and they leave a rich gummy odor in my hand that lasts for hours. I frequently detect the same odor about my hives when the bees are making all snug against the rains, or against the millers. When used by the bees, we call it propolis. Virgil refers to it as a " glue more adhesive than bird-lime and the pitch of Phrygian Ida." Pliny says it is extracted from the tears of the elm, the willow, and the reed. The bees often have serious work to detach it from their leg-baskets, and to make it stick only where they want it to.

The bud scales begin to drop in April, and by May Day the scales have fallen from the eyes of every branch in the forest. In most cases the bud has an inner wrapping that does not fall so soon. In the hickory this inner wrapping is like a great livid membrane, an inch or more in length, thick, fleshy, and shining. It clasps the tender leaves about as if both protecting and nursing them. As

187

the leaves develop, these membranous wrappings curl back, and finally wither and fall. In the plane-tree, or sycamore, this inner wrapping of the bud is a little pelisse of soft yellow or tawny fur. When it is cast off, it is the size of one's thumb-nail, and suggests the delicate skin of some golden-haired mole. The young sycamore balls lay aside their fur wrappings early in May. The flower tas-sels of the European maple, too, come packed in a slightly furry covering. The long and fleshy inner scales that enfold the flowers and leaves are of a clear olive green, thinly covered with silken hairs like the young of some animals. Our sugar maple is less striking and beautiful in the bud, but the flowers are more graceful and fringe-like.

Some trees have no bud scales. The sumac presents in early spring a mere fuzzy knot, from which, by and by, there emerges a soft, furry, tawny-colored kitten's paw. I know of nothing in vegetable nature that seems so really to be *born* as the ferns. They emerge from the ground rolled up, with a rudimentary and "touch-me-not" look, and appear to need a maternal tongue to lick them into shape. The sun plays the wet-nurse to them, and very soon they are out of that uncanny cover-ing in which they come swathed, and take their places with other green things.

The bud scales strew the ground in spring as the leaves do in the fall, though they are so small that we hardly notice them. All growth, all development, is a casting off, a leaving of something behind. First the bud scales drop, then the flower drops, then the fruit drops, then the leaf drops. The first two are preparatory and stand for spring; the last two are the crown and stand for autumn. Nearly the same thing happens with the seed in the ground. First the shell, or outer husk, is dropped or cast off; then the cotyledons, those nurse leaves of the young plant ; then the fruit falls, and at last the stalk and the leaf. A bud is a kind of seed planted in the branch instead of in the soil. It bursts and grows like a germ. In the absence of seeds and fruit, many birds and animals feed upon buds. The pine grosbeaks from the north are the most destructive budders that come among us. The snow beneath the maples they frequent is often covered with bud scales. The ruffed grouse sometimes buds in an orchard near the woods, and thus takes the farmer's apple crop a year in advance. Grafting is but a planting of buds. The seed is a complete, independent bud; it has the nutriment of the young plant within itself, as the egg holds several good lunches for the young chick. When the spider, or the wasp, or the carpenter bee, or the sand hornet lays an egg in a cell, and deposits food near it for the young when hatched, it does just what nature does in every kernel of corn or wheat, or bean, or nut. Around or within the chit or germ, she stores food for the young plant. Upon this it feeds till the root takes hold of the soil and draws sustenance from thence. The bud is rooted in the branch, and draws its sustenance from the milk of the pulpy cambium layer beneath the bark.

Another pleasant feature of spring, which I have not mentioned, is the full streams. Riding across the country one bright day in March, I saw and felt, as if for the first time, what an addition to the satisfaction one has in the open air at this season are the clear, full water-courses. They come to the front, as it were, and lure and hold the eye. There are no weeds, or grasses, or foliage to hide them; they are full to the brim, and fuller ; they catch and reflect the sunbeams, and are about the only objects of life and motion in nature. The trees stand so still, the fields are so hushed and naked, the mountains so exposed and rigid, that the eye falls upon the blue, sparkling, undulating water-courses with a peculiar satisfaction. By and by the grass and trees will be waving, and the streams will be shrunken and hidden, and our delight will not be in them. The still ponds and lakelets will then please us more.

The little brown brooks, — how swift and full they ran! One fancied something gleeful and hilarious in them. And the large creeks, — how steadily they rolled on, trailing their ample skirts along the edges of the fields and marshes, and leaving ragged patches of water here and there! Many a gentle slope spread, as it were, a turfy apron in which reposed a little pool and lakelet. Many a stream sent little detachments across lots, the sparkling water seeming to trip lightly over the unbroken turf. Here and there an oak or an elm stood knee-deep in a clear pool, as if rising from its bath. It gives one a fresh, genial feeling to see such a bountiful supply of pure, running water. One's desires and affinities go out toward the full streams. How many a parched place they reach and lap in one's memory! How many a vision of naked pebbles and sun-baked banks they cover and blot out! They give eyes to the fields; they give dimples and laughter ; they give light and motion. *Running water!* What a delightful suggestion the words always convey! One's thoughts and sympathies are set flowing by them; they unlock a fountain of pleasant fancies and associations in one's memory; the imagination is touched and refreshed.

March water is usually clean, sweet water; every brook is a trout brook, a mountain brook; the cold and the snow have supplied the condition of a high latitude; no stagnation, no corruption, comes downstream now as on a summer freshet. Winter comes down, liquid and repentant. Indeed, it is more than water that runs then: it is frost subdued; it is spring triumphant. No obsolete water-courses now. The larger creeks seek out their abandoned beds, return to the haunts of their youth, and linger fondly there. The muskrat is adrift, but not homeless; his range is vastly extended, and he evidently rejoices in full streams. Through the tunnel of the meadow-mouse the water rushes as through a pipe; and that nest of his, that was so warm and cozy beneath the snowbank in the meadow-bottom, is sodden or afloat. But meadow-mice are not afraid of water. On various occasions I have seen them swimming about the spring pools like muskrats, and, when alarmed, diving beneath the water. Add the golden willows to the full streams, with the red-shouldered starlings perched amid their branches, sending forth their strong, liquid, gurgling notes, and the picture is complete. The willow branches appear to have taken on a deeper yellow in spring; perhaps it is the effect of the stronger sunshine, perhaps it is the effect of the swift vital water laving their roots. The epaulettes of the starlings, too, are brighter than when they left us in the fall, and they appear to get brighter daily until the nesting begins. The males arrive many days before the females, and, perched along the marshes and water-courses, send forth their liquid, musical notes, passing the call from one to the other, as if to guide and hurry their mates forward.

The noise of a brook, you may observe, is by no means in proportion to its volume. The full March streams make far less noise relatively to their size than the shallower streams of summer, because the rocks and pebbles that cause the sound in summer are deeply buried beneath the current. "Still waters run deep" is not so true as "deep waters run still." I rode for half a day along the upper Delaware, and my thoughts almost unconsciously faced toward the full, clear river. Both the Delaware and the Susquehanna have a starved, impoverished look in summer, — unsightly stretches of naked drift and bare, bleaching rocks. But behold them in March, after the frost has turned over to them the moisture it has held back and stored up as the primitive forests used to hold the summer rains. Then they have an easy, ample, triumphant look, that is a feast to the eye. A plump, well-fed stream is as satisfying to behold as a well-fed animal or a thrifty tree. One source of charm in the English landscape is the full, placid stream the season through; no desiccated water-courses will you see there, nor any feeble, decrepit brooks, hardly able to get over the ground.

This condition of our streams and rivers in spring is evidently but a faint reminiscence of their condition during what we may call the geological springtime, the March or April of the earth's history, when the annual rainfall appears to have been vastly greater than at present, and when the water-courses were consequently vastly larger and fuller. In pleistocene days the earth's climate was evidently much damper than at present. It was the rainiest of March weather. On no other theory can we account for the enormous erosion of the earth's surface, and the plowing of the great valleys. Professor Newberry finds abundant evidence that the Hudson was, in former times, a much larger river than now. Professor Zittel reaches the same conclusion concerning the Nile, and Humboldt was impressed with the same fact while examining the Orinoco and the tributaries of the Amazon. All these rivers appear to be but mere fractions of their former selves. The same is true of all the great lakes. If not Noah's flood, then evidently some other very wet spell, of which this is a tradition, lies far behind us. Something like the drought of summer is beginning upon the earth; the great floods have dried up; the rivers are slowly shrinking; the water is penetrating farther and farther into the cooling crust of the earth; and what was ample to drench and cover its surface, even to make a Noah's flood, will be but a drop in the bucket to the vast interior of the cooled sphere.

X

A RIVER VIEW

A SMALL river or stream flowing by one's door has many attractions over a large body of water like the Hudson. One can make a companion of it ; he can walk with it and sit with it, or lounge on its banks, and feel that it is all his own. It becomes something private and special to him. You cannot have the same kind of attachment and sympathy with a great river; it does not flow through your affections like a lesser stream. The Hudson is a long arm of the sea, and it has something of the sea's austerity and grandeur. I think one might spend a lifetime upon its banks without feeling any sense of ownership in it, or becoming at all intimate with it: it keeps one at arm's length. It is a great highway of travel and of commerce ; ships from all parts of our seaboard plow its waters.

But there is one thing a large river does for one that is beyond the scope of the companionable streams, — it idealizes the landscape, it multiplies and heightens the beauty of the day and of the season. A fair day it makes more fair, and a wild and tempestuous day it makes more wild and tempestuous. It takes on so quickly and completely the mood and temper of the sky above. The storm is mirrored in it, and the wind chafes it into foam. The face of winter it makes doubly rigid and corpse-like. How stark and still and white it lies there! But of a bright day in spring, what life and light possess it! How it enhances or emphasizes the beauty of those calm, motionless days of summer or fall, — the broad, glassy surface perfectly duplicating the opposite shore, sometimes so smooth that the finer floating matter here and there looks like dust upon a mirror ; the becalmed sails standing this way and that, drifting with the tide. Indeed, nothing points a calm day like a great motionless sail ; it is such a conspicuous bid for the breeze which comes not.

I have observed that when the river is roily, the fact is not noticeable on a calm day; a glassy surface is a kind of mask. But when the breeze comes and agitates it a little, its real color comes out.

"Immortal water," says Thoreau, "alive to the superficies." How sensitive and tremulous and palpitating this great river is! It is only in certain lights, on certain days, that we can see how it quivers and throbs. Sometimes you can see the subtle tremor or impulse that travels in advance of the coming steamer and prophesies of its coming. Sometimes the coming of the flood-tide is heralded in the same way. Always, when the surface is calm enough and the light is favorable, the river seems shot through and through with tremblings and premonitions.

The river never seems so much a thing of life as in the spring when it first slips off its icy fetters. The dead comes to life before one's very eyes. The rigid, pallid river is resurrected in a twinkling. You look out of your window one moment, and there is that great, white, motionless expanse; you look again, and there in its place is the tender, dimpling, sparkling water. But if your eyes are sharp, you may have noticed the signs all the forenoon; the time was ripe, the river stirred a little in its icy shroud, put forth a little streak or filament of blue water near shore, made breathing-holes. Then, after a while, the ice was rent in places, and the edges crushed together or shoved one slightly upon the other ; there was apparently something growing more and more alive and restless underneath. Then suddenly the whole mass of the ice from shore to shore begins to move downstream,— very gently, almost imperceptibly at first, then with a steady, deliberate pace that soon lays bare a large expanse of bright, dancing water. The island above keeps back the northern ice, and the ebb tide makes a clean sweep from that point south for a few miles, until the return of the flood, when the ice comes back.

After the ice is once in motion, a few hours suffice to break it up pretty thoroughly. Then what a wild, chaotic scene the river presents: in one part of the day the great masses hurrying downstream, crowding and jostling each other, and struggling for the right of way; in the other, all running upstream again, as if sure of escape in that direction. Thus they race up and down, the sport of the ebb and flow; but the ebb wins each time by some distance. Large fields from above, where the men were at work but a day or two since, come down; there is their pond yet clearly defined and full of marked ice; yonder is a section of their canal partly filled with the square blocks on their way to the elevators; a piece of a race-course, or a part of a road where teams crossed, comes drifting by. The people up above have written their winter pleasure and occupations upon this page, and we read the signs as the tide bears it slowly past. Some calm, bright days the scattered and diminished masses glide by like white clouds across an April sky.

At other times, when the water is black and still, the river looks like a strip of the firmament at night, dotted with stars and moons in the shape of little and big fragments of ice. One day, I remember, there came gliding into my vision a great irregular hemisphere of ice, that vividly suggested the half moon under the telescope; its white uneven surface, pitted and cracked, the jagged inner line, the outward curve, but little broken, and the blue-black surface upon which it lay, all recalled the scenery of the midnight skies. It is only in exceptionally calm weather that the ice collects in these vast masses, leaving broad expanses of water perfectly clear. Sometimes, during such weather, it drifts by in forms that suggest the great continents, as they appear upon the map, surrounded by the oceans, all their capes and peninsulas, and isthmuses and gulfs, and inland lakes and seas, vividly reproduced.

If the opening of the river is gentle, the closing of it is sometimes attended by scenes exactly the reverse.

A cold wave one December was accompanied by a violent wind, which blew for two days and two nights. The ice formed rapidly in the river, but the wind and waves kept it from uniting and massing. On the second day the scene was indescribably wild and forbidding; the frost and fury of December were never more vividly pictured: vast crumpled, spumy ice-fields interspersed with stretches of wildly agitated water, the heaving waves thick with forming crystals, the shores piled with frozen foam and pulverized floes. After the cold wave had spent itself and the masses had become united and stationary, the scene was scarcely less wild. I fancied the plain looked more like a field of lava and scoria than like a field of ice, an eruption from some huge frost volcano of the north. Or did it suggest that a battle had been fought there, and that this wild confusion was the ruin wrought by the contending forces?

No sooner has the river pulled his icy coverlid over him than he begins to snore in his winter sleep. It is a singular sound. Thoreau calls it a "whoop," Emerson a "cannonade," and in "Merlin" speaks of

> "the gasp and moan
> Of the ice-imprisoned flood."

Sometimes it is a well-defined grunt, — *e-h-h, e-h-h*, as if some ice-god turned uneasily in his bed.

One fancies the sound is like this, when he hears it in the still winter nights seated by his fireside, or else when snugly wrapped in his own bed.

One winter the river shut up in a single night, beneath a cold wave of great severity and extent. Zero weather continued nearly a week, with a clear sky and calm, motionless air; and the effect of the brilliant sun by day and of the naked skies by night upon this vast area of new black ice, one expanding it, the other contracting, was very marked.

A cannonade indeed! As the morning advanced, out of the sunshine came peal upon peal of soft mimic thunder; occasionally becoming a regular crash, as if all the ice batteries were discharged at once. As noon approached, the sound grew to one continuous mellow roar, which lessened and became more intermittent as the day waned, until about sundown it was nearly hushed. Then, as the chill of night came on, the conditions were reversed, and the ice began to thunder under the effects of contraction; cracks opened from shore to shore, and grew to be two or three inches broad under the shrinkage of the ice. On the morrow the expansion of the ice often found vent in one of these cracks; the two edges would first crush together, and then gradually overlap each other for two feet or more.

This expansive force of the sun upon the ice is sometimes enormous. I have seen the ice explode with a loud noise and a great commotion in the water, and a huge crack shoot like a thunderbolt from shore to shore, with its edges overlapping and shivered into fragments.

When unprotected by a covering of snow, the ice, under the expansive force of the sun, breaks regularly, every two or three miles, from shore to shore. The break appears as a slight ridge, formed by the edges of the overlapping ice.

This icy uproar is like thunder, because it seems to proceed from something in swift motion; you cannot locate it; it is everywhere and yet nowhere. There is something strange and phantom-like about it. To the eye all is still and rigid, but to the ear all is in swift motion.

This crystal cloud does not open and let the bolt leap forth, but walk upon it and you see the ice shot through and through in every direction with shining, iridescent lines where the force passed. These lines are not cracks which come to the surface, but spiral paths through the ice, as if the force that made them went with a twist like a rifle bullet. In places several of them run together, when they make a track as broad as one's hand.

Sometimes, when I am walking upon the ice and this sound flashes by me, I fancy it is· like the stroke of a gigantic skater, one who covers a mile at a stride and makes the crystal floor ring beneath him. I hear his long tapering stroke ring out just beside me, and then in a twinkling it is half a mile away.

A fall of snow, and this icy uproar is instantly hushed, the river sleeps in peace. The snow is like a coverlid, which protects the ice from the changes of temperature of the air, and brings repose to its uneasy spirit.

A dweller upon its banks, I am an interested spectator of the spring and winter harvests which its waters yield. In the stern winter nights, it is a pleasant thought that a harvest is growing down there on those desolate plains which will bring work to many needy hands by and by, and health and comfort to the great cities some months later. When the nights are coldest, the ice grows as fast as corn in July. It is a crop that usually takes two or three weeks to grow, and, if the water is very roily or brackish, even longer. Men go out from

time to time and examine it, as the farmer goes out
and examines his grain or grass, to see when it will
do to cut. If there comes a deep fall of snow
before the ice has attained much thickness, it is
" pricked," so as to let the water up through and
form snow-ice. A band of fifteen or twenty men,
about a yard apart, each armed with a chisel-bar
and marching in line, puncture the ice at each step
with a single sharp thrust. To and fro they go,
leaving a belt behind them that presently becomes
saturated with water. But ice, to be first quality,
must grow from beneath, not from above. It is a
crop quite as uncertain as any other. A good yield
every two or three years, as they say of wheat out
West, is about all that can be counted on. When
there is an abundant harvest, after the ice-houses
are filled, they stack great quantities of it, as the
farmer stacks his surplus hay.

The cutting and gathering of the ice enlivens
these broad, white, desolate fields amazingly. One
looks down upon the busy scene as from a hill-top
upon a river meadow in haying time, only here the
figures stand out much more sharply than they do
from a summer meadow. There is the broad,
straight, blue-black canal emerging into view, and
running nearly across the river; this is the highway
that lays open the farm. On either side lie the
fields or ice-meadows, each marked out by cedar or
hemlock boughs. The farther one is cut first, and,

when cleared, shows a large, long, black parallelogram in the midst of the plain of snow. Then the next one is cut, leaving a strip or tongue of ice between the two for the horses to move and turn upon. Sometimes nearly two hundred men and boys, with numerous horses, are at work at once, marking, plowing, planing, scraping, sawing, hauling, chiseling ; some floating down the pond on great square islands towed by a horse, or their fellow-workmen; others distributed along the canal, bending to their ice-hooks; others upon the bridges, separating the blocks with their chisel-bars; others feeding the elevators; while knots and straggling lines of idlers here and there look on in cold discontent, unable to get a job.

The best crop of ice is an early crop. Late in the season, or after January, the ice is apt to get " sunstruck," when it becomes " shaky," like a piece of poor timber. The sun, when he sets about destroying the ice, does not simply melt it from the surface, — that were a slow process; but he sends his shafts into it and separates it into spikes and needles, — in short, makes kindling-wood of it; so as to consume it the quicker.

One of the prettiest sights about the ice-harvesting is the elevator in operation. When all works well, there is an unbroken procession of the great crystal blocks slowly ascending this incline. They go up in couples, arm in arm, as it were, like friends up a stairway, glowing and changing in the sun, and recalling the precious stones that adorned the walls of the celestial city. When they reach the platform where they leave the elevator, they seem to step off like things of life and volition; they are still in pairs, and separate only as they enter upon the " runs." But here they have an ordeal to pass through, for they are subjected to a rapid inspection by a man with a sharp eye in his head and a sharp ice-hook in his hand, and the black sheep are separated from the flock; every square with a trace of sediment or earth-stain in it, whose texture is not the perfect and unclouded crystal, is rejected, and sent hurling down into the abyss. Those that pass the examination glide into the building along the gentle incline, and are switched off here and there upon branch runs, and distributed to all parts of the immense interior. When the momentum becomes too great, the blocks run over a board full of nails or spikes, that scratch their bottoms and retard their progress, giving the looker-on an uncomfortable feeling.

A beautiful phenomenon may at times be witnessed on the river in the morning after a night of extreme cold. The new black ice is found to be covered with a sudden growth of frost ferns, — exquisite fern-like formations from a half inch to an inch in length, standing singly and in clusters, and under the morning sun presenting a most novel appearance. They impede the skate, and are presently broken down and blown about by the wind.

The scenes and doings of summer are counterfeited in other particulars upon these crystal plains. Some bright, breezy day you casually glance down the river and behold a sail, — a sail like that of a pleasure yacht of summer. Is the river open again below there? is your first half-defined inquiry. But with what unwonted speed the sail is moving across the view! Before you have fairly drawn another breath it has turned, unperceived, and is shooting with equal swiftness in the opposite direction. Who ever saw such a lively sail! It does not bend before the breeze, but darts to and fro as if it moved in a vacuum, or like a shadow over a screen. Then you remember the ice-boats, and you open your eyes to the fact. Another and another come into view around the elbow, turning and flashing in the sun, and hurtling across each other's path like white-winged gulls. They turn so quickly, and dash off again at such speed, that they produce the illusion of something singularly light and intangible. In fact, an ice-boat is a sort of disembodied yacht; it is a sail on skates. The only semblance to a boat is the sail and the rudder. The platform under which the skates or runners — three in number — are rigged is broad and low; upon this the pleasure-seekers, wrapped in their furs or blankets, lie at full length, and, looking under the sail, skim the frozen surface with their eyes. The speed attained is sometimes very great, — more than a mile per minute, and sufficient to carry them ahead of the fastest express train. When going at this rate the boat will leap like a greyhound, and thrilling stories are told of the fearful crevasses, or open places in the ice, that are cleared at a bound. And yet withal she can be brought up to the wind so suddenly as to shoot the unwary occupants off, and send them skating on their noses some yards.

Navigation on the Hudson stops about the last of November. There is usually more or less floating ice by that time, and the river may close very abruptly. Beside that, new ice an inch or two thick is the most dangerous of all ; it will cut through a vessel's hull like a knife. In 1875 there was a sudden fall of the mercury the 28th of November. The hard and merciless cold came down upon the naked earth with great intensity. On the 29th the ground was a rock, and, after the sun went down, the sky all around the horizon looked like a wall of chilled iron. The river was quickly covered with great floating fields of smooth, thin ice. About three o'clock the next morning — the mercury two degrees below zero — the silence of our part of the river was suddenly broken by the alarm bell of a passing steamer; she was in the jaws of the icy legions, and was crying for help; many sleepers alongshore remembered next day that the sound of a bell had floated across their dreams, without arousing them. One man was awakened before long by a loud pounding at his door. On opening it, a tall form, wet and icy, fell in upon him with the cry, " The Sunnyside is sunk!" The man proved to be one of her officers, and was in quest of help. He had made his way up a long hill through the darkness, his wet clothes freezing upon him, and his strength gave way the moment succor was found. Other dwellers in the vicinity were aroused, and with their boats rendered all the assistance possible. The steamer sank but a few yards from shore, only a part of her upper deck remaining above water, yet a panic among the passengers — the men behaving very badly — swamped the boats as they were being filled with the women, and a dozen or more persons were drowned.

. When the river is at its wildest, usually in March, the eagles appear. They prowl about amid the icefloes, alighting upon them or flying heavily above them in quest of fish, or a wounded duck or other game.

I have counted ten of these noble birds at one time, some seated grim and motionless upon cakes of ice, — usually surrounded by crows, — others flapping along, sharply scrutinizing the surface beneath. Where the eagles are, there the crows do congregate. The crow follows the eagle, as the jackal follows the lion, in hope of getting the leavings of the royal table. Then I suspect the crow is a real hero-worshiper. I have seen a dozen or more of them sitting in a circle about an eagle upon the ice, all with their faces turned toward him, and apparently in silent admiration of the dusky king.

The eagle seldom or never turns his back upon a storm. I think he loves to face the wildest elemental commotion. I shall long carry the picture of one I saw floating northward on a large raft of ice one day, in the face of a furious gale of snow. He stood with his talons buried in the ice, his head straight out before him, his closed wings showing their strong elbows, — a type of stern defiance and power.

This great metropolitan river, as it were, with its floating palaces, and shores lined with villas, is thus an inlet and a highway of the wild and the savage. The wild ducks and geese still follow it north in spring, and south in the fall. The loon pauses in his migrations and disports himself in its waters. Seals and otters are occasionally seen in it.

Of the Hudson it may be said that it is a very large river for its size, — that is, for the quantity of water it discharges into the sea. Its water-shed is comparatively small, — less, I think, than that of the Connecticut.

It is a huge trough with a very slight incline, through which the current moves very slowly, and which would fill from the sea were its supplies from the mountains cut off. Its fall from Albany to the bay is only about five feet. Any object upon it, drifting with the current, progresses southward no more than eight miles in twenty-four hours. The ebb tide will carry it about twelve miles, and the flood set it back from seven to nine. A drop of water at Albany, therefore, will be nearly three weeks in reaching New York, though it will get pretty well pickled some days earlier.

Some rivers by their volume and impetuosity penetrate the sea, but here the sea is the aggressor, and sometimes meets the mountain water nearly halfway.

This fact was illustrated a few years ago, when the basin of the Hudson was visited by one of the most severe droughts ever known in this part of the State. In the early winter, after the river was frozen over above Poughkeepsie, it was discovered that immense numbers of fish were retreating upstream before the slow encroachment of the salt water. There was a general exodus of the finny tribes from the whole lower part of the river ; it was like the spring and fall migration of the birds, or the fleeing of the population of a district before some approaching danger ; vast swarms of catfish, white and yellow perch, and striped bass were *en route* for the fresh water farther north. When the people alongshore made the discovery, they turned out as they do in the rural districts when the pigeons appear, and, with small gillnets let down through holes in the ice, captured them in fabulous numbers. On the heels of the retreating perch and catfish came the denizens of salt water, and codfish were taken ninety miles above New York. When the February thaw came, and brought up the volume of fresh water again, the sea brine was beaten back, and the fish, what were left of them, resumed their old feeding-grounds.

It is this character of the Hudson, this encroachment of the sea upon it, that has led Professor Newberry to speak of it as a drowned river. We have heard of drowned lands, but here is a river overflowed and submerged in the same manner. It is quite certain, however, that this has not always been the character of the Hudson. Its great trough bears evidence of having been worn to its present dimensions by much swifter and stronger currents than those that course through it now. Hence Professor Newberry has advanced the bold and striking theory that in pre-glacial times this part of the continent was several hundred feet higher than at present, and that the Hudson was then a very large and rapid stream, that drew its main supplies from the basin of the Great Lakes through an ancient river-bed that followed pretty nearly the line of the present Mohawk; in other words, that the waters of the St. Lawrence once found an outlet through this channel, debouching into the ocean

from a broad, littoral plain, at a point eighty miles
southeast of New York, where the sea now rolls
five hundred feet deep. According to the sound-
ings of the coast survey, this ancient bed of the
Hudson is distinctly marked upon the ocean floor
to the point indicated.

To the gradual subsidence of this part of the
continent, in connection with the great changes
wrought by the huge glacier that crept down from
the north during what is called the ice period, is
owing the character and aspects of the Hudson as
we see and know them. The Mohawk valley was
filled up by the drift, and the pent-up waters of
the Great Lakes found an opening through what is
now the St. Lawrence. The trough of the Hudson
was also partially filled, and has remained so to
the present day. There is, perhaps, no point in the
river where the mud and clay are not from two to
three times as deep as the water.

That ancient and grander Hudson lies back of us
several hundred thousand years, — perhaps more,
for a million years are but as one tick of the time-
piece of the Lord; yet even *it* was a juvenile compared with some of the rocks and mountains the
Hudson of to-day mirrors. The Highlands date
from the earliest geological age, — the primary; the
river — the old river — from the latest, the ter-
tiary; and what that difference means in terrestrial
years hath not entered into the mind of man to

conceive. Yet how the venerable mountains open their ranks for the stripling to pass through. Of course the river did not force its way through this barrier, but has doubtless found an opening there of which it has availea itself, and which it has enlarged.

In thinking of these things, one only has to allow time enough, and the most stupendous changes in the topography of the country are as easy and natural as the going out or the coming in of spring or summer. According to the authority above referred to, that part of our coast that flanks the mouth of the Hudson is still sinking at the rate of a few inches per century, so that in the twinkling of a hundred thousand years or so the sea will completely submerge the city of New York, the top of Trinity Church steeple alone standing above the flood. We who live so far inland, and sigh for the salt water, need only to have a little patience, and we shall wake up some fine morning and find the surf beating upon our doorsteps.

XI

BIRD ENEMIES

HOW surely the birds know their enemies!
See how the wrens and robins and bluebirds
pursue and scold the cat, while they take little or
no notice of the dog! Even the swallow will fight
the cat, and, relying too confidently upon its powers
of flight, sometimes swoops down so near to its
enemy that it is caught by a sudden stroke of the
cat's paw. The only case I know of in which our
small birds fail to recognize their enemy is furnished
by the shrike ; apparently the little birds do not
know that this modest-colored bird is an assassin.
At least I have never seen them scold or molest
him, or utter any outcries at his presence, as they
usually do at birds of prey. Probably it is because
the shrike is a rare visitant, and is not found in this
part of the country during the nesting season of our
songsters.

But the birds have nearly all found out the trick
of the jay, and, when he comes sneaking through
the trees in May and June in quest of eggs, he is
quickly exposed and roundly abused. It is amusing to see the robins hustle him out of the tree

which holds their nest. They cry, "Thief, thief!" at the top of their voices as they charge upon him, and the jay retorts in a voice scarcely less complimentary as he makes off.

The jays have their enemies also, and need to keep an eye on their own eggs. It would be interesting to know if jays ever rob jays, or crows plunder crows; or is there honor among thieves even in the feathered tribes? I suspect the jay is often punished by birds which are otherwise innocent of nest-robbing. One season I found a jay's nest in a small cedar on the side of a wooded ridge. It held five eggs, every one of which had been punctured. Apparently some bird had driven its sharp beak through their shells, with the sole intention of destroying them, for no part of the contents of the eggs had been removed. It looked like a case of revenge; as if some thrush or warbler, whose nest had suffered at the hands of the jays, had watched its opportunity, and had in this way retaliated upon its enemies. An egg for an egg. The jays were lingering near, very demure and silent, and probably ready to join a crusade against nest-robbers.

The great bugaboo of the birds is the owl. The owl snatches them from off their roosts at night, and gobbles up their eggs and young in their nests. He is a veritable ogre to them, and his presence fills them with consternation and alarm.

One season, to protect my early cherries, I placed

216

a large stuffed owl amid the branches of the tree. Such a racket as there instantly began about my grounds is not pleasant to think upon! The orioles and robins fairly "shrieked out their affright." The news instantly spread in every direction, and apparently every bird in town came to see that owl in the cherry-tree, and every bird took a cherry, so that I lost more fruit than if I had left the owl indoors. With craning necks and horrified looks the birds alighted upon the branches, and between their screams would snatch off a cherry, as if the act was some relief to their outraged feelings.

The chirp and chatter of the young of birds which build in concealed or inclosed places, like the woodpeckers, the house wren, the high-hole, the oriole, is in marked contrast to the silence of the fledgelings of most birds that build open and exposed nests. The young of the sparrows, — unless the social sparrow be an exception, — warblers, flycatchers, thrushes, never allow a sound to escape them and, on the alarm note of their parents being heard, sit especially close and motionless, while the young of chimney swallows, woodpeckers, and orioles are very noisy. The latter, in their deep pouch, are quite safe from birds of prey, except perhaps from the owl. The owl, I suspect, thrusts its leg into the cavities of woodpeckers and into the pocket-like nest of the oriole, and clutches and brings forth the birds in its talons. In one case which I heard of, a screech owl had thrust its claw into a cavity in a tree, and grasped the head of a red-headed woodpecker; being apparently unable to draw its prey forth, it had thrust its own round head into the hole, and in some way became fixed there, and had thus died with the woodpecker in its talons.

The life of birds is beset with dangers and mishaps of which we know little. One day, in my walk, I came upon a goldfinch with the tip of one wing securely fastened to the feathers of its rump by what appeared to be the silk of some caterpillar. The bird, though uninjured, was completely crippled, and could not fly a stroke. Its little body was hot and panting in my hands, as I carefully broke the fetter. Then it darted swiftly away with a happy cry. A record of all the accidents and tragedies of bird life for a single season would show many curious incidents. A friend of mine opened his box stove one fall to kindle a fire in it, when he beheld in the black interior the desiccated forms of two bluebirds. The birds had probably taken refuge in the chimney during some cold spring storm, and had come down the pipe to the stove, from whence they were unable to ascend. A peculiarly touching little incident of bird life occurred to a caged female canary. Though unmated, she laid some eggs, and the happy bird was so carried away by her feelings that she would offer food to the eggs, and chatter

and twitter, trying, as it seemed, to encourage them
to eat! The incident is hardly tragic, neither is it
comic.

Certain birds nest in the vicinity of our houses
and outbuildings, or even in and upon them, for
protection from their enemies, but they often thus
expose themselves to a plague of the most deadly
character.

I refer to the vermin with which their nests often
swarm, and which kill the young before they are
fledged. In a state of nature this probably never
happens; at least I never have seen or heard of it
happening to nests placed in trees or under rocks.
It is the curse of civilization falling upon the birds
which come too near man. The vermin, or the
germ of the vermin, is probably conveyed to the
nest in hen's feathers, or in straws and hairs picked
up about the barn or hen-house. A robin's nest
upon your porch or in your summer-house will
occasionally become an intolerable nuisance from
the swarms upon swarms of minute vermin with
which it is filled. The parent birds stem the tide as
long as they can, but are often compelled to leave
the young to their terrible fate.

One season a phœbe-bird built on a projecting
stone under the eaves of the house, and all appeared
to go well till the young were nearly fledged, when
the nest suddenly became a bit of purgatory. The
birds kept their places in their burning bed till they

could hold out no longer, when they leaped forth and fell dead upon the ground.

After a delay of a week or more, during which I imagine the parent birds purified themselves by every means known to them, the couple built another nest a few yards from the first, and proceeded to rear a second brood; but the new nest developed into the same bed of torment that the first did, and the three young birds, nearly ready to fly, perished as they sat within it. The parent birds then left the place as if it had been accursed.

I imagine the smaller birds have an enemy in our native white-footed mouse, though I have not proof enough to convict him. But one season the nest of a chickadee which I was observing was broken up in a position where nothing but a mouse could have reached it. The bird had chosen a cavity in the limb of an apple-tree which stood but a few yards from the house. The cavity was deep, and the entrance to it, which was ten feet from the ground, was small. Barely light enough was admitted, when the sun was in the most favorable position, to enable one to make out the number of eggs, which was six, at the bottom of the dim interior. While one was peering in and trying to get his head out of his own light, the bird would startle him by a queer kind of puffing sound. She would not leave her nest like most birds, but really tried to blow, or scare, the intruder away; and after repeated experiments I could hardly refrain from jerking my head back when that little explosion of sound came up from the dark interior. One night, when incubation was about half finished, the nest was harried. A slight trace of hair or fur at the entrance led me to infer that some small animal was the robber. A weasel might have done it, as they sometimes climb trees, but I doubt if either a squirrel or a rat could have passed the entrance.

Probably few persons have ever suspected the catbird of being an egg-sucker; I do not know that she has ever been accused of such a thing, but there is something uncanny and disagreeable about her, which I at once understood when I one day caught her in the very act of going through a nest of eggs.

A pair of the least flycatchers, the bird which says *chebec, chebec*, and is a small edition of the pewee, one season built their nest where I had them for many hours each day under my observation. The nest was a very snug and compact structure placed in the forks of a small maple about twelve feet from the ground. The season before, a red squirrel had harried the nest of a wood thrush in this same tree, and I was apprehensive that he would serve the flycatchers the same trick; so, as I sat with my book in a summer-house near by, I kept my loaded gun within easy reach. One egg was laid, and the next morning, as I made my daily inspection of the nest, only a fragment of its empty shell was to be found. This I removed, mentally imprecating the rogue of a red squirrel. The birds were much disturbed by the event, but did not desert the nest, as I had feared they would, but after much inspection of it, and many consultations together, concluded, it seems, to try again. Two more eggs were laid, when one day I heard the birds utter a sharp cry, and on looking up I saw a catbird perched upon the rim of the nest, hastily devouring the eggs. I soon regretted my precipitation in killing her, because such interference is generally unwise. It turned out that she had a nest of her own with five eggs, in a spruce-tree near my window.

Then this pair of little flycatchers did what I had never seen birds do before : they pulled the nest to pieces and rebuilt it in a peach-tree not many rods away, where a brood was successfully reared. The nest was here exposed to the direct rays of the noonday sun, and, to shield her young when the heat was greatest, the mother bird would stand above them with wings slightly spread, as other birds have been known to do under like circumstances.

To what extent the catbird is a nest-robber I have no evidence; but that feline mew of hers, and that flirting, flexible tail, suggest something not entirely bird-like.

BIRD ENEMIES

Probably the darkest tragedy of the nest is enacted when a snake plunders it. All birds and animals, so far as I have observed, behave in a peculiar manner toward a snake. They seem to feel something of the same loathing toward it that the human species experience. The bark of a dog when he encounters a snake is different from that which he gives out on any other occasion; it is a note of mingled alarm, inquiry, and disgust.

One day a tragedy was enacted a few yards from where I was sitting with a book: two song sparrows were trying to defend their nest against a black snake. The curious, interrogating note of a chicken who had suddenly come upon the scene in his walk first caused me to look up from my reading. There were the sparrows, with wings raised in a way peculiarly expressive of horror and dismay, rushing about a low clump of grass and bushes. Then, looking more closely, I saw the glistening form of the black snake, and the quick movement of his head as he tried to seize the birds. The sparrows darted about and through the grass and weeds, try-ing to beat the snake off. Their tails and wings were spread, and, panting with the heat and the desperate struggle, they presented a most singu-lar spectacle. They uttered no cry, not a sound escaped them ; they were plainly speechless with horror and dismay. Not once did they drop their wings, and the peculiar expression of those uplifted palms, as it were, I shall never forget. It occurred to me that perhaps here was a case of attempted bird-charming on the part of the snake, so I looked on from behind the fence. The birds charged the snake and harassed him from every side, but were evidently under no spell save that of courage in defending their nest. Every moment or two I could see the head and neck of the serpent make a sweep at the birds, when the one struck at would fall back, and the other would renew the assault from the rear. There appeared to be little danger that the snake could strike and hold one of the birds, though I trembled for them, they were so bold and approached so near to the snake's head. Time and again he sprang at them, but without success. How the poor things panted, and held up their wings appealingly! Then the snake glided off to the near fence, barely escaping the stone which I hurled at him. I found the nest rifled and deranged; whether it had contained eggs or young, I know not. The male sparrow had cheered me many a day with his song, and I blamed myself for not having rushed at once to the rescue, when the arch enemy was upon him. There is probably little truth in the popular notion that snakes charm birds. The black snake is the most subtle, alert, and devilish of our snakes, and I have never seen him have any but young, helpless birds in his mouth.

We have one parasitical bird, the cowbird, so

called because it walks about amid the grazing cattle and seizes the insects which their heavy tread sets going, which is an enemy of most of the smaller birds. It drops its egg in the nest of the song sparrow, the social sparrow, the snowbird, the vireo, and the wood-warbler, and as a rule it is the only egg in the nest that issues successfully. Either the eggs of the rightful owner of the nest are not hatched, or else the young are overridden and overreached by the parasite, and perish prematurely.

Among the worst enemies of our birds are the so-called "collectors," men who plunder nests and murder their owners in the name of science. Not the genuine ornithologist, for no one is more careful of squandering bird life than he; but the sham ornithologist, the man whose vanity or affectation happens to take an ornithological turn. He is seized with an itching for a collection of eggs and birds because it happens to be the fashion, or because it gives him the air of a man of science. But in the majority of cases the motive is a mercenary one; the collector expects to sell these spoils of the groves and the orchards. Robbing nests and killing birds becomes a business with him. He goes about it systematically, and becomes an expert in circumventing and slaying our songsters. Every town of any considerable size is infested with one or more of these bird highwaymen, and every nest in the country round about that the wretches can lay

hands on is harried. Their professional term for a
nest of eggs is a "clutch," a word that well expresses the work of their grasping, murderous fingers. They clutch and destroy in the germ the life
and music of the woodlands. Certain of our natural
history journals are mainly organs of communica-
tion between these human weasels. They record
their exploits at nest-robbing and bird-slaying in
their columns. One collector tells with gusto how
he "worked his way" through an orchard, ransack-
ing every tree and leaving, as he believed, not one
nest behind him. He had better not be caught
working his way through my orchard. Another
gloats over the number of Connecticut warblers —
a rare bird — he killed in one season in Massachu-
setts. Another tells how a mockingbird appeared
in southern New England and was hunted down
by himself and friend, its eggs "clutched," and the
bird killed. Who knows how much the bird-lovers
of New England lost by that foul deed! The progeny of the birds would probably have returned to
Connecticut to breed, and their progeny, or a part
of them, the same, till in time the famous Southern
songster would have become a regular visitant to
New England. In the same journal still another
collector describes minutely how he outwitted three
hummingbirds and captured their nests and eggs,
— a clutch he was very proud of. A Massachu-
setts bird-harrier boasts of his clutch of the eggs

of that dainty little warbler, the blue yellow-back.
One season he took two sets, the next five sets, the
next four sets, beside some single eggs, and the
next season four sets, and says he might have found
more had he had more time. One season he took,
in about twenty days, three sets from one tree. I
have heard of a collector who boasted of having
taken one hundred sets of the eggs of the marsh
wren in a single day; of another who took, in the
same time, thirty nests of the yellow-breasted chat;
and of still another who claimed to have taken
one thousand sets of eggs of different birds in one
season. A large business has grown up under the
influence of this collecting craze. One dealer in
eggs has those of over five hundred species. He
says that his business in 1883 was twice that of
1882; in 1884 it was twice that of 1883, and so
on. Collectors vie with each other in the extent
and variety of their cabinets. They not only obtain
eggs in sets, but aim to have a number of sets of
the same bird, so as to show all possible variations.
I hear of a private collection that contains twelve
sets of kingbirds' eggs, eight sets of house wrens'
eggs, four sets of mockingbirds' eggs, etc.; sets of
eggs taken in low trees, high trees, medium trees;
spotted sets, dark sets, plain sets, and light sets
of the same species of bird. Many collections are
made on this latter plan.

Thus are our birds hunted and cut off, and all

in the name of science; as if science had not long
ago finished with these birds. She has weighed
and measured and dissected and described them,
and their nests and eggs, and placed them in her
cabinet ; and the interest of science and of humanity now demands that this wholesale nest-robbing cease. These incidents I have given above, it
is true, are but drops in the bucket, but the bucket
would be more than full if we could get all the
facts. Where one man publishes his notes, hundreds, perhaps thousands, say nothing, but go as
silently about their nest-robbing as weasels.

It is true that the student of ornithology often
feels compelled to take bird life. It is not an easy
matter to "name all the birds without a gun,"
though an opera-glass will often render identifica-
tion entirely certain, and leave the songster un-
harmed; but, once having mastered the birds, the
true ornithologist leaves his gun at home. This
view of the case may not be agreeable to that desiccated mortal called the " closet naturalist," but for
my own part the closet naturalist is a person with
whom I have very little sympathy. He is about
the most wearisome and profitless creature in existence. With his piles of skins, his cases of eggs,
his laborious feather-splitting, and his outlandish
nomenclature, he is not only the enemy of the birds,
but the enemy of all those who would know them
rightly.

BIRD ENEMIES

Not the collectors alone are to blame for the diminishing numbers of our wild birds, but a large share of the responsibility rests upon quite a different class of persons, namely, the milliners. False taste in dress is as destructive to our feathered friends as are false aims in science. It is said that the traffic in the skins of our brighter-plumaged birds, arising from their use by the milliners, reaches to hundreds of thousands annually. I am told of one middleman who collected from the shooters in one district, in four months, seventy thousand skins. It is a barbarous taste that craves this kind of ornamentation. Think of a woman or girl of real refinement appearing upon the street with her head-gear adorned with the scalps of our songsters!

It is probably true that the number of our birds destroyed by man is but a small percentage of the number cut off by their natural enemies; but it is to be remembered that those he destroys are in addition to those thus cut off, and that it is this extra or artificial destruction that disturbs the balance of nature. The operation of natural causes keeps the birds in check, but the greed of the collectors and milliners tends to their extinction.

I can pardon a man who wishes to make a collection of eggs and birds for his own private use, if he will content himself with one or two specimens of a kind, though he will find any collection much less satisfactory and less valuable than he imagines;

but the professional nest-robber and skin-collector should be put down, either by legislation or with dogs and shotguns.

I have remarked above that there is probably very little truth in the popular notion that snakes can "charm" birds. But two of my correspondents have each furnished me with an incident from his own experience which seems to confirm the popular belief. One of them writes from Georgia as follows : —

"Some twenty-eight years ago I was in Calaveras County, California, engaged in cutting lumber. One day, in coming out of the camp or cabin, my attention was attracted to the curious action of a quail in the air, which, instead of flying low and straight ahead as usual, was some fifty feet high, flying in a circle, and uttering cries of distress. I watched the bird and saw it gradually descend, and following with my eye in a line from the bird to the ground, saw a large snake with head erect and some ten or twelve inches above the ground, and mouth wide open, and, as far as I could see, gazing intently on the quail (I was about thirty feet from the snake). The quail gradually descended, its circles growing smaller and smaller, and all the time uttering cries of distress, until its feet were within two or three inches of the mouth of the snake, when I threw a stone, and, though not hitting the snake, yet struck the ground so near as to frighten

him, and he gradually started off. The quail,
however, fell to the ground, apparently lifeless. I
went forward and picked it up, and found it was
thoroughly overcome with fright, its little heart
beating as if it would burst through the skin.
After holding it in my hand a few moments it flew
away. I then tried to find the snake, but could
not. I am unable to say whether the snake was
venomous, or belonged to the constricting family,
like the black snake. I can well recollect it was
large and moved off rather slow. As I had never
seen anything of the kind before, it made a great
impression on my mind, and, after the lapse of so
long a time, the incident appears as vivid to me as
though it had occurred yesterday."

It is not probable that the snake had its mouth
open; its darting tongue may have given that impression.

The other incident comes to me from Vermont.
"While returning from church in 1876," says the
writer, "as I was crossing a bridge . . . I noticed
a striped snake in the act of charming a song
sparrow. They were both upon the sand beneath
the bridge. The snake kept his head swaying
slowly from side to side and darted his tongue out
continually. The bird, not over a foot away, was
facing the snake, hopping from one foot to the
other, and uttering a dissatisfied little chirp. I
watched them till the snake seized the bird, having

gradually drawn nearer. As he seized it, I leaped over the side of the bridge; the snake glided away, and I took up the bird, which he had dropped. It was too frightened to try to fly, and I carried it nearly a mile before it flew from my open hand."

If these observers are quite sure of what they saw, then undoubtedly snakes have the power to draw birds within their grasp. I remember that my mother once told me that while gathering wild strawberries she had on one occasion come upon a bird fluttering about the head of a snake as if held there by a spell. On her appearance, the snake lowered its head and made off, and the panting bird flew away. A neighbor of mine killed a black snake which had swallowed a full-grown red squirrel, probably captured by the same power of fascination.

XII

PHASES OF FARM LIFE

I HAVE thought that a good test of civilization, perhaps one of the best, is country life. Where country life is safe and enjoyable, where many of the conveniences and appliances of the town are joined to the large freedom and large benefits of the country, a high state of civilization prevails. Is there any proper country life in Spain, in Mexico, in the South American States? Man has always dwelt in cities, but he has not always in the same sense been a dweller in the country. Rude and barbarous people build cities. Hence, paradoxical as it may seem, the city is older than the country. Truly, man made the city, and after he became sufficiently civilized, not afraid of solitude, and knew on what terms to live with nature, God promoted him to life in the country. The necessities of defense, the fear of enemies, built the first city, built Athens, Rome, Carthage, Paris. The weaker the law, the stronger the city. After Cain slew Abel he went out and built a city, and murder or the fear of murder, robbery or the fear of robbery, have built most of the cities since. Penetrate into the heart of Africa, and you will find the people, or tribes, all living in villages or little cities. You step from the jungle or the forest into the town; there is no country. The best and most hopeful feature in any people is undoubtedly the instinct that leads them to the country and to take root there, and not that which sends them flocking to the town and its distractions.

The lighter the snow, the more it drifts; and the more frivolous the people, the more they are blown by one wind or another into towns and cities.

The only notable exception I recall to city life preceding country life is furnished by the ancient Germans, of whom Tacitus says that they had no cities or contiguous settlements. "They dwell scattered and separate, as a spring, a meadow, or a grove may chance to invite them. Their villages are laid out, not like ours [the Romans] in rows of adjoining buildings, but every one surrounds his house with a vacant space, either by way of security, or against fire, or through ignorance of the art of building."

These ancient Germans were indeed true countrymen. Little wonder that they overran the empire of the city-loving Romans, and finally sacked Rome itself. How hairy and hardy and virile they were! In the same way is the more fresh and vigorous blood of the country always making eruptions into the city. The Goths and Vandals from the woods and the farms, — what would Rome do without them, after all? The city rapidly uses men up; families run out, man becomes sophisticated and feeble. A fresh stream of humanity is always setting from the country into the city; a stream not so fresh flows back again into the country, a stream for the most part of jaded and pale humanity. It is arterial blood when it flows in, and venous blood when it comes back.

A nation always begins to rot first in its great cities, is indeed perhaps always rotting there, and is saved only by the antiseptic virtues of fresh supplies of country blood.

But it is not of country life in general that I am to speak, but of some phases of farm life, and of farm life in my native State.

Many of the early settlers of New York were from New England, Connecticut perhaps sending out the most. My own ancestors were from the latter State. The Connecticut emigrant usually made his first stop in our river counties, Putnam, Dutchess, or Columbia. If he failed to find his place there, he made another flight to Orange, to Delaware, or to Schoharie County, where he generally stuck. But the State early had one element introduced into its rural and farm life not found farther east, namely, the Holland Dutch. These gave features more or less picturesque to the country that are not observable in New England. The

Dutch took root at various points along the Hudson, and about Albany and in the Mohawk valley, and remnants of their rural and domestic architecture may still be seen in these sections of the State. A Dutch barn became proverbial. " As broad as a Dutch barn " was a phrase that, when applied to the person of a man or woman, left room for little more to be said. The main feature of these barns was their enormous expansion of roof. It was a comfort to look at them, they suggested such shelter and protection. The eaves were very low and the ridge-pole very high. Long rafters and short posts gave them a quaint, short-waisted, grandmotherly look. They were nearly square, and stood very broad upon the ground. Their form was doubtless suggested by the damper climate of the Old World, where the grain and hay, instead of being packed in deep solid mows, used to be spread upon poles and exposed to the currents of air under the roof. Surface and not cubic capacity is more important in these matters in Holland than in this country. Our farmers have found that, in a climate where there is so much weather as with us, the less roof you have the better. Roofs will leak, and cured hay will keep sweet in a mow of any depth and size in our dry atmosphere.

The Dutch barn was the most picturesque barn that has been built, especially when thatched with straw, as they nearly all were, and forming one side of an inclosure of lower roofs or sheds also covered with straw, beneath which the cattle took refuge from the winter storms. Its immense, unpainted gable, cut with holes for the swallows, was like a section of a respectable-sized hill, and its roof like its slope. Its great doors always had a hood projecting over them, and the doors themselves were divided horizontally into upper and lower halves; the upper halves very frequently being left open, through which you caught a glimpse of the mows of hay, or the twinkle of flails when the grain was being threshed.

The old Dutch farmhouses, too, were always pleasing to look upon. They were low, often made of stone, with deep window-jambs and great family fireplaces. The outside door, like that of the barn, was always divided into upper and lower halves. When the weather permitted, the upper half could stand open, giving light and air without the cold draught over the floor where the children were playing that our wide-swung doors admit. This feature of the Dutch house and barn certainly merits preservation in our modern buildings.

The large, unpainted timber barns that succeeded the first Yankee settlers' log stables were also picturesque, especially when a lean-to for the cow-stable was added, and the roof carried down with a long sweep over it ; or when the barn was flanked by an open shed with a hayloft above it, where the hens cackled and hid their nests, and from the open window of which the hay was always hanging.

Then the great timbers of these barns and the Dutch barn, hewn from maple or birch or oak trees from the primitive woods, and put in place by the combined strength of all the brawny arms in the neighborhood when the barn was raised, — timbers strong enough and heavy enough for docks and quays, and that have absorbed the odors of the hay and grain until they look ripe and mellow and full of the pleasing sentiment of the great, sturdy, bountiful interior! The " big beam " has become smooth and polished from the hay that has been pitched over it, and the sweaty, sturdy forms that have crossed it. One feels that he would like a piece of furniture — a chair, or a table, or a writing-desk, a bedstead, or a wainscoting — made from these long-seasoned, long-tried, richly toned timbers of the old barn. But the smart-painted, natty barn that follows the humbler structure, with its glazed windows, its ornamented ventilator and gilded weather vane, — who cares to contemplate it? The wise human eye loves modesty and humility; loves plain, simple structures; loves the unpainted barn that took no thought of itself, or the dwelling that looks inward and not outward ; is offended when the farm-buildings get above their business and aspire to be something on their own account, suggesting, not cattle and crops and plain living, but the vanities of the town and the pride of dress and equi-page.

Indeed, the picturesque in human affairs and occupations is always born of love and humility, as it is in art or literature; and it quickly takes to itself wings and flies away at the advent of pride, or any selfish or unworthy motive. The more directly the farm savors of the farmer, the more the fields and buildings are redolent of human care and toil, without any thought of the passer-by, the more we delight in the contemplation of it.

It is unquestionably true that farm life and farm scenes in this country are less picturesque than they were fifty or one hundred years ago. This is owing partly to the advent of machinery, which enables the farmer to do so much of his work by proxy, and hence removes him farther from the soil, and partly to the growing distaste for the occupation among our people. The old settlers — our fathers and grandfathers — loved the farm, and had no thoughts above it ; but the later generations are looking to the town and its fashions, and only waiting for a chance to flee thither. Then pioneer life is always more or less picturesque ; there is no room for vain and foolish thoughts; it is a hard battle, and the people have no time to think about appearances. When my grandfather and grandmother came into the country where they reared their family and passed their days, they cut a road through the woods and brought all their worldly gear on a sled drawn by a yoke of oxen. Their neighbors helped them build a house of logs, with a roof of black-ash bark and a floor of hewn white-ash plank. A great stone chimney and fireplace — the mortar of red clay — gave light and warmth, and cooked the meat and baked the bread, when there was any to cook or to bake. Here they lived and reared their family, and found life sweet. Their unworthy descendant, yielding to the inherited love of the soil, flees the city and its artificial ways, and gets a few acres in the country, where he proposes to engage in the pursuit supposed to be free to every American citizen, — the pursuit of happiness. The humble old farmhouse is discarded, and a smart, modern country-house put up. Walks and roads are made and graveled; trees and hedges are planted; the rustic old barn is rehabilitated; and, after it is all fixed, the uneasy proprietor stands off and looks, and calculates by how much he has missed the picturesque, at which he aimed. Our new houses undoubtedly have greater comforts and conveniences than the old ; and, if we could keep our pride and vanity in abeyance and forget that all the world is looking on, they might have beauty also.

The man that forgets himself, he is the man we like; and the dwelling that forgets itself, in its purpose to shelter and protect its inmates and make

them feel at home in it, is the dwelling that fills the
eye. When you see one of the great cathedrals,
you know that it was not pride that animated these
builders, but fear and worship; but when you see
the house of the rich farmer, or of the millionaire
from the city, you see the pride of money and the
insolence of social power.

Machinery, I say, has taken away some of the
picturesque features of farm life. How much so-
ever we may admire machinery and the faculty
of mechanical invention, there is no machine like
a man; and the work done directly by his hands,
the things made or fashioned by them, have a
virtue and a quality that cannot be imparted by
machinery. The line of mowers in the meadows,
with the straight swaths behind them, is more picturesque than the "Clipper" or "Buckeye" mower,
with its team and driver. So are the flails of the
threshers, chasing each other through the air, more
pleasing to the eye and the ear than the machine,
with its uproar, its choking clouds of dust, and its
general hurly-burly.

Sometimes the threshing was done in the open
air, upon a broad rock, or a smooth, dry plat of
greensward; and it is occasionally done there yet,
especially the threshing of the buckwheat crop, by
a farmer who has not a good barn floor, or who
cannot afford to hire the machine. The flail makes
a louder *thud* in the fields than you would imagine;

241

and in the splendid October weather it is a pleasing spectacle to behold the gathering of the ruddy crop, and three or four lithe figures beating out the grain with their flails in some sheltered nook, or some grassy lane lined with cedars. When there are three flails beating together, it makes lively music; and when there are four, they follow each other so fast that it is a continuous roll of sound, and it requires a very steady stroke not to hit or get hit by the others. There is just room and time to get your blow in, and that is all. When one flail is upon the straw, another has just left it, another is halfway down, and the fourth is high and straight in the air. It is like a swiftly revolving wheel that delivers four blows at each revolution. Threshing, like mowing, goes much easier in company than when alone; yet many a farmer or laborer spends nearly all the late fall and winter days shut in the barn, pounding doggedly upon the endless sheaves of oats and rye.

When the farmers made "bees," as they did a generation or two ago much more than they do now, a picturesque element was added. There was the stone bee, the husking bee, the "raising," the "moving," etc. When the carpenters had got the timbers of the house or the barn ready, and the foundation was prepared, then the neighbors for miles about were invited to come to the "raisin'." The afternoon was the time chosen. The forenoon was occupied by the carpenter and the farm hands in putting the sills and " sleepers " in place ("sleepers," what a good name for those rude hewn timbers that lie under the floor in the darkness and silence!). When the hands arrived, the great beams and posts and joists and braces were carried to their place on the platform, and the first " bent," as it was called, was put together and pinned by oak pins that the boys brought. Then pike poles were distributed, the men, fifteen or twenty of them, arranged in a line abreast of the bent; the boss carpenter steadied and guided the corner post and gave the word of command, — " Take holt, boys!" " Now, set her up!" " Up with her!" " Up she goes!" When it gets shoulder high, it becomes heavy, and there is a pause. The pikes are brought into requisition; every man gets a good hold and braces himself, and waits for the words. " All together now!" shouts the captain; " Heave her up!" " He-o-he!" (heave-all, — heave), " he-o-he," at the top of his voice, every man doing his best. Slowly the great timbers go up; louder grows the word of command, till the bent is up. Then it is plumbed and stay-lathed, and another is put together and raised in the same way, till they are all up. Then comes the putting on the great plates, — timbers that run lengthwise of the building and match the sills below. Then, if there is time, the putting up of the rafters.

In every neighborhood there was always some

man who was especially useful at "raisin's." He was bold and strong and quick. He helped guide and superintend the work. He was the first one up on the bent, catching a pin or a brace and putting it in place. He walked the lofty and perilous plate with the great beetle in hand, put the pins in the holes, and, swinging the heavy instrument through the air, drove the pins home. He was as much at home up there as a squirrel.

Now that balloon frames are mainly used for houses, and lighter sawed timbers for barns, the old-fashioned raising is rarely witnessed.

Then the moving was an event, too. A farmer had a barn to move, or wanted to build a new house on the site of the old one, and the latter must be drawn to one side. Now this work is done with pulleys and rollers by a few men and a horse; then the building was drawn by sheer bovine strength. Every man that had a yoke of cattle in the country round about was invited to assist. The barn or house was pried up and great runners, cut in the woods, placed under it, and under the runners were placed skids. To these runners it was securely chained and pinned; then the cattle — stags, steers, and oxen, in two long lines, one at each runner — were hitched fast, and, while men and boys aided with great levers, the word to go was given. Slowly the two lines of bulky cattle straightened and settled into their bows; the big chains that wrapped

the runners tightened, a dozen or more " gads "
were flourished, a dozen or more lusty throats urged
their teams at the top of their voices, when there
was a creak or a groan as the building stirred.
Then the drivers redoubled their efforts; there was
a perfect Babel of discordant sounds; the oxen bent
to the work, their eyes bulged, their nostrils distended; the lookers-on cheered, and away went the
old house or barn as nimbly as a boy on a hand-
sled. Not always, however; sometimes the chains
would break, or one runner strike a rock, or bury
itself in the earth. There were generally enough
mishaps or delays to make it interesting.

In the section of the State of which I write, flax
used to be grown, and cloth for shirts and trousers,
and towels and sheets, woven from it. It was no
laughing matter for the farm-boy to break in his
shirt or trousers, those days. The hair shirts in
which the old monks used to mortify the flesh could
not have been much before them in this mortifying
particular. But after the bits of shives and sticks
were subdued, and the knots humbled by use and
the washboard, they were good garments. If you
lost your hold in a tree and your shirt caught on a
knot or limb, it would save you.

But when has any one seen a crackle, or a swin-
gling-knife, or a hetchel, or a distaff, and where can
one get some tow for strings or for gun-wadding, or
some swingling-tow for a bonfire ? The quill-wheel,

and the spinning-wheel, and the loom are heard
no more among us. The last I knew of a certain
hetchel, it was nailed up behind the old sheep that
did the churning ; and when he was disposed to
shirk or hang back and stop the machine, it was
always ready to spur him up in no uncertain manner. The old loom became a hen-roost in an out-
building; and the crackle upon which the flax was
broken, — where, oh, where is it ?

When the produce of the farm was taken a long
distance to market, — that was an event, too; the
carrying away of the butter in the fall, for instance,
to the river, a journey that occupied both ways
four days. Then the family marketing was done
in a few groceries. Some cloth, new caps and boots
for the boys, and a dress, or a shawl, or a cloak for
the girls were brought back, besides news and adventure, and strange tidings of the distant world.
The farmer was days in getting ready to start; food
was prepared and put in a box to stand him on the
journey, so as to lessen the hotel expenses, and
oats were put up for the horses. The butter was
loaded up overnight, and in the cold November
morning, long before it was light, he was up and off.
I seem to hear the wagon yet, its slow rattle over the
frozen ground diminishing in the distance. On the
fourth day toward night all grew expectant of his return, but it was usually dark before his wagon was
heard coming down the hill, or his voice from before

246

the door summoning a light. When the boys got big enough, one after the other accompanied him each year, until all had made the famous journey and seen the great river and the steamboats, and the thousand and one marvels of the far-away town. When it came my turn to go, I was in a great state of excitement for a week beforehand, for fear my clothes would not be ready, or else that it would be too cold, or else that the world would come to an end before the time fixed for starting. The day previous I roamed the woods in quest of game to supply my bill of fare on the way, and was lucky enough to shoot a partridge and an owl, though the latter I did not take. Perched high on a "spring-board" I made the journey, and saw more sights and wonders than I have ever seen on a journey since, or ever expect to again.

But now all this is changed. The railroad has found its way through or near every settlement, and marvels and wonders are cheap. Still, the essential charm of the farm remains and always will remain: the care of crops, and of cattle, and of orchards, bees, and fowls; the clearing and improving of the ground; the building of barns and houses; the direct contact with the soil and with the elements; the watching of the clouds and of the weather; the privacies with nature, with bird, beast, and plant; and the close acquaintance with the heart and virtue of the world. The farmer should be the true naturalist ; the book in which it is all written is open before him night and day, and how sweet and wholesome all his knowledge is!

The predominant feature of farm life in New York, as in other States, is always given by some local industry of one kind or another. In many of the high, cold counties in the eastern centre of the State, this ruling industry is hop-growing; in the western, it is grain and fruit growing; in sections along the Hudson, it is small-fruit growing, as berries, currants, grapes; in other counties, it is milk and butter; in others, quarrying flagging-stone. I recently visited a section of Ulster County, where everybody seemed getting out hoop-poles and making hoops. The only talk was of hoops, hoops! Every team that went by had a load or was going for a load of hoops. The principal fuel was hoop-shavings or discarded hoop-poles. No man had any money until he sold his hoops. When a farmer went to town to get some grain, or a pair of boots, or a dress for his wife, he took a load of hoops. People stole hoops and poached for hoops, and bought, and sold, and speculated in hoops. If there was a corner, it was in hoops; big hoops, little hoops, hoops for kegs, and firkins, and barrels, and hogsheads, and pipes; hickory hoops, birch hoops, ash hoops, chestnut hoops, hoops enough to go around the world. Another place it was shingle, shingle; everybody was shaving hemlock shingle.

PHASES OF FARM LIFE

In most of the eastern counties of the State, the interest and profit of the farm revolve about the cow. The dairy is the one great matter, — for milk, when milk can be shipped to the New York market, and for butter when it cannot. Great barns and stables and milking-sheds, and immense meadows and cattle on a thousand hills, are the prominent agricultural features of these sections of the country. Good grass and good water are the two indispensables to successful dairying. And the two generally go together. Where there are plenty of copious cold springs, there is no dearth of grass. When the cattle are compelled to browse upon weeds and various wild growths, the milk and butter will betray it in the flavor. Tender, juicy grass, the ruddy blossoming clover, or the fragrant, well-cured hay, make the delicious milk and the sweet butter. Then there is a charm about a natural pastoral country that belongs to no other. Go through Orange County in May and see the vivid emerald of the smooth fields and hills. It is a new experience of the beauty and effectiveness of simple grass. And this grass has rare virtues, too, and imparts a flavor to the milk and butter that has made them famous.

Along all the sources of the Delaware the land flows with milk, if not with honey. The grass is excellent, except in times of protracted drought, and then the browsings in the beech and birch

249

woods are a good substitute. Butter is the staple product. Every housewife is or wants to be a famous butter-maker, and Delaware County butter rivals that of Orange in market. Delaware is a high, cool grazing country. The farms lie tilted up against the sides of the mountain or lapping over the hills, striped or checked with stone walls, and presenting to the eye long stretches of pasture and meadow land, alternating with plowed fields and patches of waving grain. Few of their features are picturesque ; they are bare, broad, and simple. The farmhouse gets itself a coat of white paint, and green blinds to the windows, and the barn and wagon-house a coat of red paint with white trimmings, as soon as possible. A penstock flows by the doorway, rows of tin pans sun themselves in the yard, and the great wheel of the churning-machine flanks the milk-house, or rattles behind it. The winters are severe, the snow deep. The principal fuel is still wood, — beech, birch, and maple. It is hauled off the mountain in great logs when the first November or December snows come, and cut up and piled in the wood-houses and under a shed. Here the axe still rules the winter, and it may be heard all day and every day upon the wood-pile, or echoing through the frost-bound wood, the coat of the chopper hanging to a limb, and his white chips strewing the snow.

Many cattle need much hay ; hence in dairy sections haying is the period of " storm and stress " in the farmer's year. To get the hay in, in good condition, and before the grass gets too ripe, is a great matter. All the energies and resources of the farm are bent to this purpose. It is a thirty or forty days' war, in which the farmer and his "hands" are pitted against the heat and the rain and the legions of timothy and clover. Everything about it has the urge, the hurry, the excitement of a battle. Outside help is procured; men flock in from adjoining counties, where the ruling industry is something else and is less imperative; coopers, blacksmiths, and laborers of various kinds drop their tools, and take down their scythes and go in quest of a job in haying. Every man is expected to pitch his endeavors in a little higher key than at any other kind of work. The wages are extra, and the work must correspond. The men are in the meadow by half-past four or five in the morning, and mow an hour or two before breakfast. A good mower is proud of his skill. He does not " lop in," and his " pointing out " is perfect, and you can hardly see the ribs of his swath. He stands up to his grass and strikes level and sure. He will turn a double down through the stoutest grass, and when the hay is raked away you will not find a spear left standing. The Americans are — or were — the best mowers. A foreigner could never quite give the masterly touch. The hayfield has its code. One

man must not take another's swath unless he expects to be crowded. Each expects to take his turn
leading the band. The scythe may be so whetted
as to ring out a saucy challenge to the rest. It is
not good manners to mow up too close to your
neighbor, unless you are trying to keep out of the
way of the man behind you. Many a race has been
brought on by some one being a little indiscreet in
this respect. Two men may mow all day together
under the impression that each is trying to put
the other through. The one that leads strikes out
briskly, and the other, not to be outdone, follows
close. Thus the blood of each is soon up; a little
heat begets more heat, and it is fairly a race before
long. It is a great ignominy to be mowed out of
your swath. Hay-gathering is clean, manly work
all through. Young fellows work in haying who do
not do another stroke on the farm the whole year.
It is a gymnasium in the meadows and under
the summer sky. How full of pictures, too! — the
smooth slopes dotted with cocks with lengthening
shadows; the great, broad-backed, soft-cheeked
loads, moving along the lanes and brushing under
the trees; the unfinished stacks with forkfuls of
hay being handed up its sides to the builder, and
when finished the shape of a great pear, with a
pole in the top for the stem. Maybe in the fall and
winter the calves and yearlings will hover around
it and gnaw its base until it overhangs them and

shelters them from the storm. Or the farmer will "fodder" his cows there, — one of the most picturesque scenes to be witnessed on the farm, — twenty or thirty or forty milchers filing along toward the stack in the field, or clustered about it, waiting the promised bite. In great, green flakes the hay is rolled off, and distributed about in small heaps upon the unspotted snow. After the cattle have eaten, the birds — snow buntings and red-polls — come and pick up the crumbs, the seeds of the grasses and weeds. At night the fox and the owl come for mice.

What a beautiful path the cows make through the snow to the stack or to the spring under the hill! — always more or less wayward, but broad and firm, and carved and indented by a multitude of rounded hoofs.

In fact, the cow is the true pathfinder and pathmaker. She has the leisurely, deliberate movement that insures an easy and a safe way. Follow her trail through the woods, and you have the best, if not the shortest, course. How she beats down the brush and briers and wears away even the roots of the trees! A herd of cows left to themselves fall naturally into single file, and a hundred or more hoofs are not long in smoothing and compacting almost any surface.

Indeed, all the ways and doings of cattle are pleasant to look upon, whether grazing in the pas-

ture, or browsing in the woods, or ruminating under
the trees, or feeding in the stall, or reposing upon
the knolls. There is virtue in the cow; she is full
of goodness; a wholesome odor exhales from her;
the whole landscape looks out of her soft eyes; the
quality and the aroma of miles of meadow and pasture lands are in her presence and products. I had
rather have the care of cattle than be the keeper
of the great seal of the nation. Where the cow is,
there is Arcadia; so far as her influence prevails,
there is contentment, humility, and sweet, homely
life.

Blessed is he whose youth was passed upon the
farm, and if it was a dairy farm, his memories will
be all the more fragrant. The driving of the cows
to and from the pasture, every day and every season
for years, — how much of summer and of nature
he got into him on these journeys! What rambles
and excursions did this errand furnish the excuse
for! The birds and birds'-nests, the berries, the
squirrels, the woodchucks, the beech woods with
their treasures into which the cows loved so to
wander and to browse, the fragrant wintergreens
and a hundred nameless adventures, all strung upon
that brief journey of half a mile to and from the
remote pastures. Sometimes a cow or two will
be missing when the herd is brought home at
night; then to hunt them up is another adventure.
My grandfather went out one night to look up an

absentee from the yard, when he heard something in the brush, and out stepped a bear into the path before him.

Every Sunday morning the cows were salted. The farm-boy would take a pail with three or four quarts of coarse salt, and, followed by the eager herd, go to the field and deposit the salt in handfuls upon smooth stones and rocks and upon clean places on the turf. If you want to know how good salt is, see a cow eat it. She gives the true saline smack. How she dwells upon it, and gnaws the sward and licks the stones where it has been deposited! The cow is the most delightful feeder among animals. It makes one's mouth water to see her eat pumpkins, and to see her at a pile of apples is distracting. How she sweeps off the delectable grass! The sound of her grazing is appetizing; the grass betrays all its sweetness and succulency in parting under her sickle.

The region of which I write abounds in sheep also. Sheep love high, cool, breezy lands. Their range is generally much above that of cattle. Their sharp noses will find picking where a cow would fare poorly indeed. Hence most farmers utilize their high, wild, and mountain lands by keeping a small flock of sheep. But they are the outlaws of the farm and are seldom within bounds. They make many lively expeditions for the farm-boy, — driving them out of mischief, hunting them up in the mountains, or salting them on the breezy hills. Then there is the annual sheep-washing, when on a warm day in May or early June the whole herd is driven a mile or more to a suitable pool in the creek, and one by one doused and washed and rinsed in the water. We used to wash below an old grist-mill, and it was a pleasing spectacle, — the mill, the dam, the overhanging rocks and trees, the round, deep pool, and the huddled and frightened sheep.

One of the features of farm life peculiar to this country, and one of the most picturesque of them all, is sugar-making in the maple woods in spring. This is the first work of the season, and to the boys is more play than work. In the Old World, and in more simple and imaginative times, how such an occupation as this would have got into literature, and how many legends and associations would have clustered around it! It is woodsy, and savors of the trees; it is an encampment among the maples. Before the bud swells, before the grass springs, before the plow is started, comes the sugar harvest. It is the sequel of the bitter frost; a sap-run is the sweet good-by of winter. It denotes a certain equipoise of the season; the heat of the day fully balances the frost of the night. In New York and New England, the time of the sap hovers about the vernal equinox, beginning a week or ten days before, and continuing a week or ten days after As the days and nights get equal, the heat and cold

256

get equal, and the sap mounts. A day that brings the bees out of the hive will bring the sap out of the maple-tree. It is the fruit of the equal marriage of the sun and the frost. When the frost is all out of the ground, and all the snow gone from its surface, the flow stops. The thermometer must not rise above 38° or 40° by day, or sink below 24° or 25° at night, with wind in the northwest; a relaxing south wind, and the run is over for the present. Sugar weather is crisp weather. How the tin buckets glisten in the gray woods; how the robins laugh; how the nuthatches call; how lightly the thin blue smoke rises among the trees! The squirrels are out of their dens; the migrating water-fowls are streaming northward; the sheep and cattle look wistfully toward the bare fields; the tide of the season, in fact, is just beginning to rise.

Sap-letting does not seem to be an exhaustive process to the trees, as the trees of a sugar-bush appear to be as thrifty and as long-lived as other trees. They come to have a maternal, large-waisted look, from the wounds of the axe or the auger, and that is about all.

In my sugar-making days, the sap was carried to the boiling-place in pails by the aid of a neck-yoke and stored in hogsheads, and boiled or evaporated in immense kettles or caldrons set in huge stone arches ; now, the hogshead goes to the trees hauled upon a sled by a team, and the sap is evaporated in broad, shallow, sheet-iron pans, — a great saving of fuel and of labor.

Many a farmer sits up all night boiling his sap, when the run has been an extra good one, and a lonely vigil he has of it amid the silent trees and beside his wild hearth. If he has a sap-house, as is now so common, he may make himself fairly comfortable; and if a companion, he may have a good time or a glorious wake.

Maple sugar in its perfection is rarely seen, perhaps never seen, in the market. When made in large quantities and indifferently, it is dark and coarse; but when made in small quantities — that is, quickly from the first run of sap and properly treated — it has a wild delicacy of flavor that no other sweet can match. What you smell in freshly cut maple-wood, or taste in the blossom of the tree, is in it. It is then, indeed, the distilled essence of the tree. Made into syrup, it is white and clear as clover-honey; and crystallized into sugar, it is as pure as the wax. The way to attain this result is to evaporate the sap under cover in an enameled kettle; when reduced about twelve times, allow it to settle half a day or more; then clarify with milk or the white of an egg. The product is virgin syrup, or sugar worthy the table of the gods.

Perhaps the most heavy and laborious work of the farm in the section of the State of which I write is fence-building. But it is not unproductive labor, as in the South or West, for the fence is of stone, and the capacity of the soil for grass or grain is, of course, increased by its construction. It is killing two birds with one stone: a fence is had, the best in the world, while the available area of the field is enlarged. In fact, if there are ever sermons in stones, it is when they are built into a stone wall, — turning your hindrances into helps, shielding your crops behind the obstacles to your husbandry, making the enemies of the plow stand guard over its products. This is the kind of farming worth imitating. A stone wall with a good rock bottom will stand as long as a man lasts. Its only enemy is the frost, and it works so gently that it is not till after many years that its effect is perceptible. An old farmer will walk with you through his fields and say, " This wall I built at such and such a time, or the first year I came on the farm, or when I owned such and such a span of horses," indicating a period thirty, forty, or fifty years back. " This other, we built the summer so and so worked for me," and he relates some incident, or mishap, or comical adventures that the memory calls up. Every line of fence has a history; the mark of his plow or his crowbar is upon the stones; the sweat of his early manhood put them in place; in fact, the long black line covered with lichens and in places tottering to the fall revives long-gone scenes and events in the life of the farm.

The time for fence-building is usually between seed-time and harvest, May and June; or in the fall after the crops are gathered. The work has its picturesque features, — the prying of rocks; supple forms climbing or swinging from the end of the great levers; or the blasting of the rocks with powder, the hauling of them into position with oxen or horses, or with both; the picking of the stone from the greensward; the bending, athletic forms of the wall-layers; the snug new fence creeping slowly up the hill or across the field, absorbing the windrow of loose stones; and, when the work is done, much ground reclaimed to the plow and the grass, and a strong barrier erected.

It is a common complaint that the farm and farm life are not appreciated by our people. We long for the more elegant pursuits, or the ways and fashions of the town. But the farmer has the most sane and natural occupation, and ought to find life sweeter, if less highly seasoned, than any other. He alone, strictly speaking, has a home. How can a man take root and thrive without land? He writes his history upon his field. How many ties, how many resources, he has, — his friendships with his cattle, his team, his dog, his trees, the satisfaction in his growing crops, in his improved fields; his intimacy with nature, with bird and beast, and with the quickening elemental forces; his coöperations with the clouds, the sun, the seasons, heat, wind, rain, frost ! Nothing will take the various social distempers which the city and artificial life breed out of a man like farming, like direct and loving contact with the soil. It draws out the poison. It humbles him, teaches him patience and reverence, and restores the proper tone to his system.

Cling to the farm, make much of it, put yourself into it, bestow your heart and your brain upon it, so that it shall savor of you and radiate your virtue after your day's work is done!

"Be thou diligent to know the state of thy flocks, and look well to thy herds.

"For riches are not forever; and doth the crown endure to every generation ?

"The hay appeareth, and the tender grass showeth itself, and herbs of the mountains are gathered.

"The lambs are for thy clothing, and the goats are the price of the field.

"And thou shalt have goat's milk enough for thy food, for the food of thy household, and for the maintenance for thy maidens."

XIII

ROOF–TREE

ONE of the greatest pleasures of life is to build a house for one's self. There is a peculiar satisfaction even in planting a tree from which you hope to eat the fruit, or in the shade of which you hope to repose. But how much greater the pleasure in planting the roof-tree, the tree that bears the golden apples of home and hospitality, and under the protection of which you hope to pass the remainder of your days! My grandmother said the happiest day of her life was when she found herself mistress of a little log-house in the woods. Grandfather and she had built it mainly with their own hands, and doubtless with as much eagerness and solicitude as the birds build their nests. It was made of birch and maple logs, the floor was of hewn logs, and its roof of black-ash bark. But it was home and fireside, a few square feet of the great, wild, inclement, inhospitable out of doors subdued and set about by four walls and made warm and redolent of human hearts. I notice how eager all men are in building their houses, how they linger about them, or even about their proposed sites.

When the cellar is being dug, they want to take a hand in it; the earth evidently looks a little different, a little more friendly and congenial, than other earth. When the foundation walls are up and the first floor is rudely sketched by rough timbers, I see them walking pensively from one imaginary room to another, or sitting long and long, wrapped in sweet reverie, upon the naked joist. It is a favorite pastime to go there of a Sunday afternoon and linger fondly about: they take their friends or their neighbors and climb the skeleton stairs and look out of the vacant windows, and pass in and out of the just sketched doorways. How long the house is a-finishing! The heart moves in long before the workmen move out. Will the mason and the painter and the plumber never be through?

When a new house is going up in my vicinity, I find myself walking thitherward nearly every day to see how the work progresses. What pleasure to see the structure come into shape, and the architect's paper plans take form and substance in wood and stone! I like to see every piece fitted, every nail driven. I stand about till I am in the way of the carpenters or masons. Another new roof to shelter somebody from the storms, another four walls to keep the great cosmic out of doors at bay!

Though there is pleasure in building our house, or in seeing our neighbor build, yet the old houses look the best. Disguise it as one will, the new house is more or less a wound upon nature, and time must elapse for the wound to heal. Then, unless one builds with modesty and simplicity, and with a due regard to the fitness of things, his house will always be a wound, an object of offense upon the fair face of the landscape. Indeed, to build a house that shall not offend the wise eye, that shall not put Nature and all her gentle divinities to shame, is the great problem. In such matters, not to displease the eye is to please the heart.

Probably the most that is to be aimed at in domestic architecture is negative beauty, a condition of things which invites or suggests beauty to those who are capable of the sentiment, because a house, truly viewed, is but a setting, a background, and is not to be pushed to the front and made much of for its own sake. It is for shelter, for comfort, for health and hospitality, to eat in and sleep in, to be born in and to die in, and it is to accord in appearance with homely every-day usages, and with natural, universal objects and scenes. Indeed, is anything but negative beauty to be aimed at in the interior decorations as well? The hangings are but a background for the pictures, and are to give tone and atmosphere to the rooms; while the whole interior is but a background for the human form, and for the domestic life to be lived there.

It may be observed that what we call beauty of nature is mainly negative beauty; that is, the mass, the huge rude background, made up of rocks, trees, hills, mountains, plains, water, has not beauty as a positive quality, visible to all eyes, but affords the mind the conditions of beauty, namely, health, strength, fitness, etc., beauty being an *experience* of the beholder. Some things, on the other hand, as flowers, foliage, brilliant colors, sunsets, rainbows, waterfalls, may be said to be beautiful in and of themselves; but how wearisome the world would be without the vast negative background upon which these things figure, and which provokes and stimulates the mind in a way the purely fair forms do not!

How we are drawn by that which retreats and hides itself, or gives only glimpses and half views! Hence the value of trees as a veil to an ugly ornamental house, and the admirable setting they form to the picturesque habitation I am contemplating. But the house the heart builds, whether it be cottage or villa, can stand the broad, open light without a screen of any kind. Its neutral gray or brown tints, its wide projections and deep shadows, its simple strong lines, its coarse open-air quality, its ample roof or roofs, blend it with the landscape wherever it stands. Such a house seems to retreat into itself, and invites the eye to follow. Its interior warmth and coziness penetrate the walls, and the eye gathers suggestions of them at every point.

We can miss almost anything else from a building rather than a look of repose. This it must have. Give it a look of repose, and all else shall be added. This is the supreme virtue in architecture. Go to the city, walk up and down the principal thoroughfares, and see what an effort many of the buildings make to stand up! What columns and arches they put forth where no columns or arches are needed! There is endless variety of form and line, great activity of iron and stone, when the eye demands simplicity and repose. No broad spaces, no neutral ground. The architect in his search for variety has made his façade bristle with meaningless forms. But now and then the eye is greeted by honest simplicity of structure. Look at that massive front yonder, built of granite blocks, simply one stone on top of another from the ground to the roof, with no fuss or flutter about the openings in the walls. How easy, how simple, and what a look of dignity and repose! But probably, the next time we come this way, they will have put hollow metal hoods over the windows, or otherwise marred the ease and dignity of that front.

Doubtless one main source of the pleasure we take in a brick or stone wall over one of wood is just in this element of simplicity and repose; the structure is visible; there is nothing intricate or difficult about it. It is one stone or one brick on top of another all the way up; the building makes no effort at all to stand up, but does so in the most natural and inevitable way in the world. In a wooden building the anatomy is more or less hidden ; we do not see the sources of its strength. The same is true of a stuccoed or rough-cast building; the eye sees nothing but smooth, expressionless surface.

One great objection to the Mansard roof in the country, now happily nearly gone out of date, is that it fails to give a look of repose. It fails also to give a look of protection. The roof of a building allies it to the open air, and carries the suggestion of shelter as no other part does; and to belittle it, or conceal it, or in any way to take from the honest and direct purport of it as the shield, the main matter after all, is not to be allowed. In the city we see only the fronts, the façades of the houses; there the flat and the Mansard are less offensive. But in the country the house is individualized, stands defined, and every vital and necessary part is to be boldly and strongly treated. The Mansard gives to the country house a smart, dapper appearance, and the effect of being perked up and looking about for compliments; such houses seem to be ready to make the military salute as you pass them. Whereas the steep, high roof gives the house a settled, brooding, introverted look. It also furnishes a sort of foil to the rest of the building.

What constitutes the charm to the eye of the old-fashioned country barn but its immense roof, — a

slope of gray shingle exposed to the weather like
the side of a hill, and by its amplitude suggesting
a bounty that warms the heart? Many of the old
farmhouses, too, were modeled on the same generous
scale, and at a distance little was visible but their
great sloping roofs. They covered their inmates as
a hen covereth her brood, and are touching pictures
of the domestic spirit in its simpler forms.

What is a man's house but his nest, and why
should it not be nest-like both outside and in, —
coarse, strong, negative in tone externally, and snug
and well-feathered and modeled by the heart within?
Why should he set it on a hill, when he can command a nook under the hill or on its side? Why
should it look like an observatory, when it is a con-
servatory and dormitory?

The domestic spirit is quiet, informal, uncere-
monious, loves ease, privacy, low tones ; loves the
chimney-corner, the old armchair, the undress garb,
homely cares, children, simple pleasures ; and why
should it, when it seeks to house itself from the
weather, aim at the formal, the showy, the architectural, the external, the superfluous? Let state
edifices look stately, but the private dwelling should
express privacy and coziness.

Every man's house is in some sort an effigy of
himself. It is not the snails and shell-fish alone
that excrete their tenements, but man as well.
When you seriously build a house, you make public

proclamation of your taste and manners, or your want of these. If the domestic instinct is strong in you, and if you have humility and simplicity, they will show very plainly in your dwelling ; if you have the opposite of these, false pride or a petty ambition, or coldness and exclusiveness, they will show also. A man seldom builds better than he knows, when he assumes to know anything about it.

I think that, on examination, it will be found that the main secret of the picturesqueness of more simple structures, like fences, bridges, sheds, and log-huts, is that the *motive*, the principle of construction, is so open and obvious. No doubt much might be done to relieve the flatness of our pine-box houses by more frankness and boldness in this respect. If the eye could see more fully the necessities of the case, — how the thing stands up and is held together, that it is not pasteboard, that it does not need to be anchored against the wind, — it would be a relief. Hence the lively pleasure we feel in what are called " timber-houses," and in every architectural device by which the anatomy, the real framework, of the structure, inside or out, is allowed to show, or made to serve as ornament. The eye craves lines of strength, evidence of weight and stability. But in the wooden house, as usually treated, these lines are nearly all concealed, the ties and supports are carefully suppressed, and the eye must feed on the small, fine lines of the finish.

When the mere outlines of the frame are indicated, so that the larger spaces appear as panels, it is a great help ; or let any part of the internal economy show through, and the eye is interested, as the projection of the chimney-stack in brick or stone houses, or the separating of the upper from the main floor by a belt and slight projection, or by boldly projecting the chamber floor-joist, and letting one story overlap the other.

As I have already said, herein is the main reason of the picturesqueness of the stone house above all others. Every line is a line of strength and necessity. We see how the mass stands up ; how it is bound and keyed and fortified. The construction is visible ; the corners are locked by header and stretcher, and are towers of strength ; the openings pierce the walls and reveal their cohesion ; every stone is alive with purpose, and the whole affects one as a real triumph over Nature, — so much form and proportion wrested from her grasp. There is power in stone, and in a less measure in brick ; but wood must be boldly handled not to look frail or flat. Then unhewn stone has the negative beauty which is so desirable.

I say, therefore, build of stone by all means, if you have a natural taste to gratify, and the rockier your structure looks, the better. All things make friends with a stone house, — the mosses and lichens, and vines and birds. It is kindred to the earth and the elements, and makes itself at home in any situation.

When I set out to look up a place in the country, I was chiefly intent on finding a few acres of good fruit land near a large stone-heap. While I was yet undecided about the land, the discovery of the stone-heap at a convenient distance — vast piles of square blocks of all sizes, wedged off the upright strata by the frost during uncounted ages, and all mottled and colored by the weather — made me hasten to close the bargain. The large country-seats in the neighborhood were mainly of brick or pine ; only a few of the early settlers had availed themselves of this beautiful material that lay in such abundance handy to every man's back door, and in those cases the stones were nearly buried in white mortar, as if they were something to be ashamed of. Truly, the besmeared, beplastered appearance of most stone houses is by no means a part of their beauty. Mortar plays a subordinate part in a structure, and the less we see of it the better.

The proper way to treat the subject is this : as the work progresses, let the wall be got ready for pointing up, but never let the pointing be done, though your masons will be sorely grieved. Let the joints be made close, then scraped out, cut with the trowel, and, while the mortar is yet green, sprinkled with sand. Instead, then, of a white band defining every stone, you have only sharp lines and seams here and there, which give the wall a rocky, natural appearance.

The point of union between the stones, according to my eye, should be a depression, a shadow, and not a raised joint. So that you have closeness and compactness, the face of your wall cannot be too broken or rough. When the rising or setting sun shines athwart it, and brings out the shadows, how powerful and picturesque it looks ! It is not in cut or hewn stone to express such majesty. I like the sills and lintels of undressed stone also, — "wild stone," as the old backwoodsman called them, untamed by the hammer or chisel. If the lintels are wide enough, a sort of hood may be formed over the openings by projecting them a few inches.

It seems to me that I built into my house every one of those superb autumn days which I spent in the woods getting out stone. I did not quarry the limestone ledge into blocks any more than I quarried the delicious weather into memories to adorn my walls. Every load that was sent home carried my heart and happiness with it. The jewels I had uncovered in the débris, or torn from the ledge in the morning, I saw in the jambs, or mounted high on the corners at night. Every day was filled with great events. The woods held unknown treasures. Those elder giants, frost and rain, had wrought industriously ; now we would unearth from the leaf-mould an ugly customer, a stone with a ragged quartz face, or cavernous, and set with rock crystals like great teeth, or else suggesting a battered and worm-eaten skull of some old stone dog. These I needed a sprinkling of for their quaintness, and to make the wall a true compendium of the locality. Then we would unexpectedly strike upon several loads of beautiful blocks all in a nest ; or we would assault the ledge in a new place with wedge and bar, and rattle down headers and stretchers that surpassed any before. I had to be constantly on the lookout for corner stone, for mine is a house of seven corners, and on the strength and dignity of the corners the beauty of the wall largely depends. But when you bait your hook with your heart, the fish always bite. " The boss is as good as six men in the woods, getting out stone," flatteringly spoke up the master-mason. Certain it is that no such stone was found as when I headed the search. The men saw indifferently with their eyes, but I looked upon the ground with such desire that I saw what was beneath the moss and the leaves. With them it was hard labor at so much a day, with me it was a passionate pursuit ; the enthusiasm of the chase venting itself with the bar and the hammer, and the day was too short for me to tire of the sport.

The stone was exceptionally fine, both in form and color. Sometimes it seemed as if we had struck upon the ruins of some ancient structure, the blocks were so regular and numerous. The ancient stone-cutters, however, had shaped them all to a particular pattern, which was a little off the square; but in bringing them back with the modern pitching-tool the rock face was gained, which is the feature so desirable.

I like a live stone, one upon which time makes an impression, which in the open air assumes a certain tone and mellowness. The stone in my locality surpasses any I have ever seen in this respect. A warm gray is the ruling tint, and a wall built of this stone is of the color of the bole of the beech-tree, mottled, lively, and full of character.

What should a house of undressed stone be trimmed out with but unpainted wood? Oak, ash, cedar, cherry, maple, — why import pine from Michigan or Maine when nearly all our woods contain plenty of these materials? And now that the planing-mills are so abundant, and really do such admirable work, an ordinary-priced house may be trimmed out mainly in hard wood for nearly the same cost as with pine.

In my case I began at the stump; I viewed the trees before they were cut, and took a hand in sawing them down and in hauling them to the mill. One bleak winter day I climbed to the top of a mountain to survey a large butternut which some hunters had told me of, and which now, one year later, I see about me in base and panel as I write.

One thus gets a lively background of interest and reminiscence in his house from the start.

The natural color and grain of the wood give a richness and simplicity to an interior that no art can make up for. How the eye loves a genuine thing; how it delights in the nude beauty of the wood! A painted surface is a blank, meaningless surface; but the texture and figure of the wood is full of expression. It is the principle of construction again appearing in another field. How endless the variety of figures that appear even in one kind of wood, and, withal, how modest! The grainers do not imitate oak. They cannot. Their surface glares; their oak is only skin-deep; their figures put nature to shame.

Oak is the wood to start with in trimming a house. How clear and strong it looks! It is the master wood. When allowed to season in the log, it has a richness and ripeness of tone that are delicious. We have many kinds, as rock oak, black oak, red oak, white oak, — all equally beautiful in their place. Red oak is the softest, and less liable to spring. By combining two different kinds, as red oak and white oak (white oak takes its name from the external color of the tree, and not from the color of the wood, which is dark amber), a most pleasing effect is produced.

Butternut is the softest and most tractable of what are called hard woods, and its hue is eminently warm and mellow. Its figure is pointed and shooting, — a sort of Gothic style in the grain. It makes admirable doors. Western butternut, which can usually be had in the Albany market, makes doors as light as pine, and as little liable to spring. The Western woods are all better than the Eastern for building purposes. They are lighter, coarser, easier worked. They grow easier and thriftier. The traveler through northern Ohio and Indiana sees a wonderful crop of forest trees, tall, uniform, straight as candles, no knots, no gnarls, — all clear, clean timber. The soil is deep and moist, and the trees grow rank and rapid. The chestnut, ash, and butternut grown here work like pine, besides being darker and richer in color than the same woods grown in leaner and more rocky soils. Western black ash is especially beautiful. In connection with our almost bone-white sugar maple for panels, it makes charming doors, — just the thing for chambers, and scarcely more expensive than pine. Of our Eastern woods, red cedar is also good, with its pungent, moth-expelling odor, and should not be neglected. It soon fades, but it is very pleasing, with its hard, solid knots, even then. No doubt some wash might be applied that would preserve its color.

There is a species of birch growing upon our mountains that makes an admirable finish. It is usually called red or cherry birch, and it has a long wave or curl that is found in no other wood. It is very tough and refractory, and must be securely fastened. A black ash door, with maple or white pine panels set in a heavy frame of this red, wavy birch, is a most pleasing chamber finish. For a hard-wood floor, in connection with oak or ash, it is to be preferred to cherry.

Growing alongside of the birch is the soft maple — the curly species — that must not be overlooked. It contains light wood and dark wood, as a fowl contains white meat and dark meat. It is not unusual to find a tree of this species, the heart of which will be a rich grayish brown, suggesting, by something in the tone and texture of it, the rarer shades of silk, while the outer part is white, and fine as ivory. I have seen a wainscoting composed of alternate strips of this light and dark wood from the same tree that was exquisite, and a great rarity.

The eye soon tires of sharp, violent contrasts. In general, that which is striking or taking at first sight is to be avoided in interior finishings or decorations, especially in the main or living rooms. In halls, a more pronounced style is permissible, and the contrast of walnut with pine, or maple, or oak is more endurable. What one wants in his living-rooms is a quiet, warm tone, and the main secret of this is dark furniture and hangings, with a dash of color here and there, and floods of light, — big windows, and plenty of them. No room can be cheerful and inviting without plenty of light, and then, if the walls are light too, and the carpets showy, there is a flatness and garishness. The marble mantelpiece, with its senseless vases, and the marble-topped centre-table add the finishing touch of coldness and stiffness. Marble makes good tombstones, but it is an abomination in a house, either in furniture or in mantels.

There remains only to be added that, after you have had the experience, after the house is finished and you have had a year or two to cool off in (it takes that long), you will probably feel a slight reaction. Or it may be more than that: the scales may fall from your eyes, and you may see that it is not worth while after all to lay so much emphasis on the house, a place to shelter you from the elements, and that you have had only a different but the same unworthy pride as the rest, as if anything was not good enough, and as if manhood was not sufficient to itself without these props.

You will have found, too, that with all your pains you have not built a house, nor can you build one, that just fills the eye and gives the same æsthetic pleasure as does the plain unpainted structure that took no thought of appearances, and that has not one stroke about it foreign to the necessities of the case.

Pride, when it is conscious of itself, is death to the nobly beautiful, whether in dress, manners equipage, or house-building. The great monumental structures of the Old World show no pride or vanity, but on the contrary great humility and singleness of purpose. The Gothic cathedral does not try to look beautiful; it *is* beautiful from the start, and entirely serious. London Bridge is a heroic resolution in stone, and apparently has but one purpose, and that is to carry the paved street with all its surging masses safely over the river.

Unless, therefore, you have had the rare success of building without pride, your house will offend you by and by, and offend others.

Perhaps after one had graduated in this school and built four or five houses, he would have the courage to face the problem squarely, and build, much more plainly and unpretentiously, a low, nestling structure of undressed boards, or unhammered stone, and be content, like the oyster, with the roughest of shells without, so that he be sure of the mother-of-pearl within.

INDEX

Acorns, 13.
Adder's-tongue, 32.
Agassiz, Louis, 35.
Ancients, false science of the, 21–23.
Anemone, 182.
Ants, as weather prophets, 9.
Apples, frozen, 53, 54, 59, 143.
April, the relish of, 176; cresses in, 176, 177; arrival of birds in, 178, 179; the flowers of, 182, 183; green landscapes of, 183–186; swelling buds in, 186–190.
Arbutus, trailing, 31, 182.
Arnold, Matthew, quotation from, 170.
Ash, black, 277, 278.
Audubon, John James, 182.

Bald Mountain, 129–132.
Barns, Dutch, 236–239; old unpainted, 237, 238; modern painted, 238; building, 242–244; moving, 244, 245; roofs of, 268, 269.
Bear, black, the rifleman and the bear, 123, 124, 127; sagacity of a mother, 127, 128, 130, 131.
Bee. See Bumblebee and Honeybee.
Bee, carpenter, 189.
Beechnuts, 13.
Birch, paper or canoe, uses of, 105–109.
Birch, red or cherry, 277, 278.
Birds, winter flocks of, 65; their lives subject to many dangers, 67–69; the home instinct in, 67; dangers to early nests, 69; locations of nests, 75; position of the female among, 146; spring arrival of, 178, 179; silence and songs of migrating, 179, 180; battles between female, 181; chatter and silence of young, 217; their sufferings from vermin, 219, 220; collectors among the worst enemies of, 225, 226; milliners as the enemies of, 289; charmed by snakes, 230–232.
Birds of prey, 89.
Birthroot. See Trillium, purple.
Bitter-sweet, 13, 55.
Blackbird, red-winged. See Starling, red-shouldered.
Black-thorn, 182.
Bladder-nut, 13.
Bladderwort, horned, 29, 132.
Blind miller, a, 34.
Bloodroot, 32, 182, 186.
Blueberry, 130.
Bluebird (*Sialia sialis*), 64, 71, 97, 141; wintering in New York State, 176; battle between rival females, 181, 218; notes of, 181; nest of, 69.
Bobolink (*Dolichonyx oryzivorus*), 67, 86–88; notes of, 89; nest of, 86–88.
Bob-white. See Quail.
Bryant, William Cullen, his *Yellow Violet*, 29, 30; his hymn to the sea, 168.
Buds of trees, 186–190.
Bullfrog, 176.
Bumblebee, the sapper and miner preceding the honey-bee, 20.
Bunting, indigo. See Indigo-bird.
Bunting, snow, or snowflake (*Passerina nivalis*), 62, 135, 143, 253.

INDEX

INDEX

Farm, the, picturesque life and scenes of, 239–245; homespun garments of, 245; wheels and looms, 245, 246; taking the produce to market, 246, 247; the essential charm of, 247, 248; local industries, 248; the dairy, 249–255; haying, 250–253; sheep, 255; sugar-making, 256–258; fence-building, 258, 259; its healthful influence on the farmer, 260, 261.

Farmhouses, Dutch, 237; log, 240; modern, 240; building, 242–244; moving, 244, 245; roofs of, 260.

Fence-building, 258, 259.

Ferns, birth of, 188.

Finch, purple (*Carpodacus purpureus*), 97.

Fish, retreating up the Hudson, 210, 211.

Flagg, Wilson, quotation from, 47.

Flea, snow, 27.

Flicker. *See* High-hole.

Flycatcher, least (*Empidonax minimus*), robbed by a catbird, 222; rebuilding a nest, 222; a mother shading her young, 222; notes of, 221; nest of, 221, 222.

Fox, black *or* silver-gray, 28, 124.

Fox, red, 53, 65, 99, 124, 135; tracks of, 136, 253.

Frog. *See* Bullfrog.

Frog, piping. *See* Hyla, Pickering's.

Frog, wood, 17–19.

Frogs, as weather prophets, 13.

Fungus, phallic, 33.

Furlow Lake, 14.

Ghost-story, a, 117, 118.

Gilder, Richard Watson, his *The New Day*, 170.

Gnatcatcher, blue-gray (*Polioptila cœrulea*), nest of, 84.

Goldfinch, American, *or* yellow-bird (*Astragalinus tristis*), 62, 66, 89, 97; a curious accident, 218; nest of, 69.

Goose, wild, *or* Canada (*Branta canadensis*), 209.

Grasshoppers, in winter, 27.

Grosbeak, pine (*Pinicola enucleator leucura*), 46, 135, 143, 189.

Grouse, ruffed, *or* partridge (*Bonasa umbellus*), 51, 55, 62, 99, 135, 189.

Guide. *See* Nathan, Uncle.

Hair-bird. *See* Chippie.

Hare, northern, 99.

Harebell, 133.

Hawks, 156.

Haying, 241, 250–252.

Hemlock, the rooting of a young, 14–16; manner of growth of, 40, 41; shedding its leaves, 42, 48; beauties and uses of, 51, 52, 58.

Hepatica, 28; the first flower of spring, 182, 183; its beauty, 183; fragrance of individuals, 183.

Hetchels, 245.

Hickory, 187.

High-hole, *or* flicker (*Colaptes auratus luteus*), drumming of, 152; notes of, 152; nest of, 217.

Holmes, Oliver Wendell, 170.

Homer, quotations from, 95.

Honey-bees, 9, 20; gleaning after the bumble-bee, 20; method of filling her baskets, 20, 21; false science of the ancient observers in regard to, 21, 22; flowers visited by, 32; their first spring harvest, 178; collecting and using propolis, 187.

Honey-locust, 13.

Honeysuckle, 143.

Hoops and hoop-poles, 248.

Hornet, sand, 189.

Houses, the owners' satisfaction in building, 263, 264; negative beauty desirable in, 264–267; a look of repose desirable in, 267; roofs, 268, 269; should express privacy and coziness, 269; effigies of their owners, 269; framework should be visible in frame houses, 270, 271; picturesqueness of stone, 271, 272; proper

285

INDEX

use of mortar in stone houses, 272, 273; quarrying stone for a house, 273-275; beauties of various woods for finishing, 275-278; quiet warm colors desirable in finishings and decorations, 278, 279; simplicity, after all, most desirable in, 279, 280. *See* Farmhouses.

Hudson River, an arm of the sea, 195; calms and ripples on, 196; breaking up of the ice in, 197-199; freezing over, 199; ice cannonades on, 200, 201; snow on, 202; ice-harvesting on, 202-205; frost ferns on the ice, 205; ice-boating on, 206, 207; ice stops navigation on, 207; sinking of a steamer in, 207; eagles on, 208, 209; a highway of wild life, 209; current and tides of, 209-212; a great retreat of fish upstream, 210, 211; geological history of, 211-213.

Hugo, Victor, 40.

Humboldt, Baron von, quotations from, 7, 12, 53.

Hummingbird, ruby-throated (*Trochilus colubris*), 113; nest of, 84, 226.

Hyla, Pickering's, 176, 177.

Ice, breaking up in the Hudson, 197-199; formation on the Hudson, 199; cannonade of the, 200, 201; harvest of, 202-205; frost ferns on, 205; a steamer sunk by, 207, 208.

Ice-boats, 206, 207.

Indigo-bird, *or* indigo-bunting (*Cyanospiza cyanea*), 179.

Jay, blue (*Cyanocitta cristata*), in winter, 54, 55; hiding food, 55-57; 135, 137; a nest-robber, 215, 216; a case of revenge, 216; nest of, 216.

Junco. *See* Snowbird.

Juniper, 13.

Kingbird (*Tyrannus tyrannus*),

eggs devoured by a fish crow, 74, 75; 89, 179, 227; nest of, 74.

Kinglet, ruby-crowned (*Regulus calendula*), song of 180.

Kinglets, 64, 65.

Lady's-slipper, yellow, 29.

Lark, shore *or* horned (*Otocoris alpestris*), 62, 143.

Laurel, 55.

Linnæa, 132.

Linnet, pine, *or* pine siskin (*Spinus pinus*), 46.

Log-cock. *See* Woodpecker, pileated.

Looms, 246.

Loon (*Gavia imber*), habits and appearance of, 113-115; 208; notes of, 113, 114.

Lotus, tree. *See* Sugar-berry.

Lowell, James Russell, his *Al Fresco*, 31; quotations from, 47, 96.

Maine, camping in, 105-134.

Maple, European, 186, 188.

Maple, soft, 186; wood of, 278.

Maple, sugar, supplying food for squirrels, 59, 60; tapped by a woodpecker, 154, 155; buds and flowers of, 188; effect of tapping on, 257; wood of, 277, 278.

March, a typical day of, 6; the full streams of, 190-194.

Marigold, marsh, 186.

Meadowlark (*Sturnella magna*), in winter, 64, 68.

Merganser, 133.

Mice, wild, in winter, 62, 63, 99.

Miller, Joaquin, quotations from, 169, 170.

Millinery, barbarous, 289.

Mockingbird (*Mimus polyglottos*), 226, 227.

Moose, hunting, 124, 126.

Moth, violet-colored, 182.

Mountain-ash, 143.

Mount Bigelow, 131.

Mouse, meadow, tunnels and nests of, 192; swimming, 192.

INDEX

INDEX

INDEX

(*Dendroica cœrulescens*), a faithful mother, 80, 81; nest of, 79–81.

Warbler, blue yellow-backed *or* northern parula (*Compsothlypis americana usneœ*), 51; eggs of, 227.

Warbler, Connecticut (*Geothlypis agilis*), 226.

Warbler, yellow red-poll *or* yellow palm (*Dendroica palmarum hypochrysea*), appearance and habits of, 178; notes of, 179.

Warblers, songs of migrating, 180.

Wasp, 20, 23, 189.

Watercress, 176, 177.

Water-lily. *See* Pond-lily.

Water-thrush, Louisiana (*Seiurus motacilla*), spring arrival of, 182; song of, 182.

Waxwing, cedar. *See* Cedar-bird.

Weasel, *or* ermine, *or* stoat, habits of, 90–93, 221.

Weather signs, 7–10, 16–18.

White, Gilbert, 6, 19, 24, 115.

Whitman, Walt, quotations from, 161, 168, 170, 171; sea-salt in his poetry, 170–173.

Whittier, John Greenleaf, quotations from, 47, 48.

Willow, 186.

Willow, golden, 192.

Wilson, Alexander, 153.

Winter, familiarity of wild creatures in, 136, 137; alternation of severe and mild winters, 175; animal life in open winters, 176.

Wolf, 53.

Woodbine, 143.

Woodpecker, downy (*Dryobates pubescens medianus*), a welcome neighbor, 144; winter-quarters, 144–148, 156; an ungallant male, 145, 146; drumming of, 149–153, 156; mating, 151, 153; leaving winter-quarters, 156; nest of, 156, 157.

Woodpecker, hairy (*Dryobates villosus*), usurping a downy woodpecker's hole, 156; notes of, 156.

Woodpecker, northern pileated, *or* black log-cock (*Ceophlœus pileatus abieticola*), 133, 152; notes of, 133.

Woodpecker, red-bellied (*Melanerpes carolinus*), 153.

Woodpecker, red-headed (*Melanerpes erythrocephalus*), 57; drumming on a lightning-rod, 152, 217.

Woodpecker, yellow-bellied, *or* yellow-bellied sapsucker (*Sphyrapicus varius*), injuring fruit trees, 154, 155; tapping a maple-tree, 154, 155.

Woodpeckers, their fare in winter, 55, 61, 89; drumming habits of, 149–154; young of, 217.

Woods, struggle for life of trees in, 52; autumnal beauty of mixed, 52.

Woods, hard, for finishing houses, 275–278.

Wordsworth, William, quotation from, 36.

Wren, house (*Troglodytes aëdon*), 78, 227; nest of, 156, 217.

Yellowbird. *See* Goldfinch, American.

HARPER NATURE LIBRARY
New Paperback Editions of Outstanding Nature Classics

☐ CN 846   THE ARCTURUS ADVENTURE *by William Beebe.*
Illustrated. An account of the New York Zoological
Society's first oceanographic expedition. $5.95

☐ CN 840   SIGNS AND SEASONS *by John Burroughs. New
illustrations by Ann Zwinger.* An enduring classic from
one of the most popular nature writers of the nineteenth
century. $5.95

☐ CN 839   THE WORLD OF NIGHT *by Lorus J. and Margery
J. Milne. Illustrated by T. M. Shortt.* The fascinating
drama of nature that is enacted between dusk and dawn.
   $5.95

☐ CN 841   THE ARCTIC PRAIRIES *by Ernest Thompson Seton.
Illustrated by the author.* A canoe-journey of 2,000 miles
in search of the caribou, being the account of a voyage to
the region north of Aylmer Lake. $5.95

☐ CN 806   THE INSECT WORLD OF J. HENRI FABRE
*by J. Henri Fabre. Selected, with interpretative comments,
by Edwin Way Teale.* The best writing of J. Henri Fabre,
the great French entomologist. $5.95

☐ CN 842   BEYOND THE ASPEN GROVE *by Ann Zwinger.
Illustrated by the author.* Zwinger has written "a
collector's item that even nonbotanists will enjoy ...
a book of charm and distinction." *Library Journal* $5.95

Buy them at your local bookstore or use this handy coupon for ordering:

**HARPER & ROW, Mail Order Dept. #28CN, 10 East 53rd St., New York,
N.Y. 10022.**
Please send me the books I have checked above. I am enclosing $_____
which includes a postage and handling charge of $1.00 for the first book and 25¢
for each additional book. Send check or money order—no cash or C.O.D.'s
please.

Name _____

Address _____

City _____ State _____ Zip _____

Please allow 4 weeks for delivery. USA and Canada only. This offer expires
4/1/82. Please add any applicable sales tax.